DEVELOPING

Building on...

Achievement in Year 9 English

Jenny Thomas and Diane White

NELSON
A Cengage Company

Building On ... Achievment in Year 9 English DEVELOPING
1st Edition
Jenny Thomas
Diane White

Text and cover deign: Book Design Ltd
Typesetter: Book Design Ltd
Production controller: Siew Han Ong
Reprint: Jess Lovell
Book Design Ltd

Any URLs contained in this publication were checked for currency during the production process. Note, however, that the publisher cannot vouch for the ongoing currency of URLs.

Acknowledgements
Our grateful thanks to all past and present colleagues who have so generously shared their expertise, creativity and resources. English departments thrive on your collegiality.

The authors and publisher wish to thank the following people and organisations for permission to use the resources in this textbook. Every effort has been made to contact all copyright owners of material used in this book. In most cases this was successful and copyright is acknowledged as requested. Owners of any work reproduced here for which permission has not been cleared, please contact the publisher.

Extracts and full text (pages 62–64) from 'All Summer in a Day' by Ray Bradbury, reprinted by permission of Don Congdon Associates, Inc, copyright 1954, renewed 1982 by Ray Bradbury; page 14 S. Enright; page 16 'The Boxer' by Emma Payne; page 17 extract from 'Sunday Morning' by Lauris Edmond; page 24 newspaper article 'Ancient rituals usher in New Year' by Errol Kiong reprinted with permission from North Shore Times Jan 31, 2003; page 26 Retailworld Resourcing for the advertisement; page 28 'Dinghy at the Water's Edge' by John Geraets; page 40 The Good, the Bad and the Dusty courtesy Jet Magazine New Zealand; page 44 'Footrot Flats' cartoon strip courtesy Murray Ball, Meryl Howell; page 45 extract from G-Force courtesy Tania Roxborogh; page 50 NZ Beef and Lamb for the advertisement; page 54 'Fone Filosofy' by Louise Phyn; page 60 North Shore City Council for the 'Understanding Our Environment' advertisement; page 66 Winter and Summer in Bannockburn by Oliver Miller; Live-wire Learning (www.livewirelearning.co.nz) for selected grammar examples.

For product information and technology assistance,
in Australia call **1300 790 853**;
in New Zealand call **0800 449 725**

For permission to use material from this text or product, please email
aust.permissions@cengage.com

National Library of New Zealand Cataloguing-in-Publication Data
Thomas, Jenny.
Building on— achievement in year 9 English : developing / Jenny Thomas and Diane White.
ISBN 978-0-17-019592-8
1. English language—Rhetoric—Juvenile literature. 2. English language—Composition and exercises—Juvenile literature.
[1. English language—Rhetoric. 2. English language—Composition and exercises.] I. White, Diana. II. Title.
808.042—dc 22

Cengage Learning Australia
Level 7, 80 Dorcas Street
South Melbourne, Victoria Australia 3205

Cengage Learning New Zealand
Unit 4B Rosedale Office Park
331 Rosedale Road, Albany, North Shore 0632, NZ

For learning solutions, visit **cengage.co.nz**

Printed in China by 1010 Printing International Limited.
7 8 9 10 11 12 24

Contents

Focus 1

Focus 2

Language activities from How to ... Achieve in Year 9 English

This section connects directly to the first chapter of the accompanying textbook *How to ... Achieve in Year 9 English*. You may like to use this to make your life easier.

Group 1: Parts of Speech

Check it

A noun is a naming word. There are four main types of nouns: common, proper, abstract and collective.

Identify the **common noun(s)** in the following sentences by either circling them in blue pen or using a highlighter.

1   The athlete won the race.
2   The cyclist climbed the hill.
3   The boy plays tennis.

Identify the **proper noun(s)** in the following sentences by either circling them in blue pen or using a highlighter.

4   My sister Jennifer is a lawyer.
5   Matthew is a very good cyclist and he rides for the province of Southland.
6   Mum and Dad went to Melbourne for the Commonwealth Games last month.

Identify the **abstract noun(s)** in the following sentences by either circling them in blue pen or using a highlighter.

7   The speaker showed her concern.
8   Tania's honesty was noticed by her friends.
9   Colin has a short temper.
10   Ed's tennis shows great skill and promise.

Identify the **collective noun(s)** in the following sentences by either circling them in blue pen or using a highlighter.

11   The rugby team practised every night before the big game.
12   I went to hear the orchestra play.
13   The boy looked carefully at the photo of a pack of wolves.
14   The principal addressed his staff for the last time.

Pronouns

The pronoun takes the place of a noun.

Identify the **personal pronoun(s)** in the following sentences by either circling them in blue pen or using a highlighter.

1   Kate and I went to the circus last night.
2   At the circus we saw the juggling monkeys.
3   The boys found that the big top was full when they arrived. The tent was much bigger than us.
4   Soon the clowns came out and made us laugh at the funny tricks they did.
5   Kate and I ate popcorn while we watched the movie. It filled us up.
6   You should have seen the clever little monkey ride the bike. Kate loved him.
7   The trapeze artists were brave. They were swinging high up in the roof of the tent. It looked very dangerous.
8   Jim was the ringmaster. He was kind but the animals still obeyed him.
9   One of the clowns sat beside me and grabbed my handbag. I yelled at him and told him the handbag was mine.
10   Kate said she would join the circus if they let her.

Adjectives

Adjectives describe nouns and pronouns.

Identify the **adjective(s)** in the following sentences by either circling them in blue pen or using a highlighter.

1   He did not know what could have caused this terrible state of affairs.
2   Golan scratched his thick, red beard.
3   He wondered where to start to solve this strange mystery.
4   Just then he heard a faint, thin cry.
5   He hurried towards the solid, brick house opposite him.
6   'Hello!' he rudely shouted, as he pushed open the creaky door.
7   From out of the dusty darkness the small voice answered nervously.
8   'Are you a kind friend or nasty foe?' he asked.
9   'This dessert is really delicious,' said Mum.
10   The child spat out the sour lemon.

ISBN 9780170195928

Comparatives and superlatives

A comparative compares two things. A superlative compares more than two things and describes the best.

Identify the **comparative(s)** and **superlative(s)** in the following sentences by either circling them in blue pen or using a highlighter.

1 The children were happier than they had ever thought possible.
2 She cried out in the smallest voice imaginable.
3 The more he practised, the more competent he became.
4 The strangest thing of all was the door was still locked.
5 The weather is becoming sunnier and warmer by the day.
6 As we dived deeper, the colours and variety of sealife grew.

Verbs

A verb is a 'doing' or an 'action' word.

Identify the **verb(s)** in the following sentences by either circling them in blue pen or using a highlighter.

1 Charlotte rode her bike to the shops.
2 She entered the dairy and asked for an ice cream.
3 The ice cream was hokey-pokey and it tasted wonderful.
4 Charlotte spotted her Aunt Elisabeth across the road.
5 She waved to her and called out, 'Hi, auntie!' in a loud voice.
6 Her Aunt looked across at her and waved back.
7 'I am on my way to your house,' she said as she came close to Charlotte.

Adverbs

Adverbs are words that tell us more about verbs. They answer the question 'How?', 'When?' or 'Where?'.

Identify the **adverb(s)** in the following sentences by either circling them in blue pen or using a highlighter.

1 The boy ran quickly around the corner.
2 The very sick child was taken to the hospital.
3 Rebecca behaved stupidly.
4 The dog hungrily ate his dinner.
5 We are coming now.
6 Don't eat so quickly.
7 She crept silently towards the door.
8 I have been waiting here for 30 minutes!
9 The rain was welcome after the long drought.
10 The hikers were lost because of the heavy rain.

Conjunctions

Conjunctions are connecting words that join two or more sentences into a single sentence. They can also join words, phrases or clauses.

Identify the **conjunction(s)** in the following sentences by either circling them in blue pen or using a highlighter.

1 She speaks French and German fluently.
2 I've been learning French for five years yet I am still far from fluent.
3 Take a thermos flask and a cake of chocolate with you.
4 You can have the Holden or the Honda; it is your choice.
5 'If you can't stand the heat, get out of the kitchen,' said the politician.

Prepositions

Prepositions are the 'small words' that usually relate two words or groups of words to one another.

Identify the **preposition(s)** in the following sentences by either circling them in blue pen or using a highlighter.

1 The TV news begins at 6.00.
2 You'll find the supplementary copy on the shelf.
3 The kids were running through the bush.
4 Brittany picked up the *Dolly* magazine.
5 Statistics New Zealand conducted a census in 2005.

Let's recap parts of speech

Read the extract from the Ray Bradbury short story *All Summer in a Day* below and complete the activities that follow:

> But she remembered and stood quietly apart from all of them and watched the patterning windows. And once, a month ago, she had refused to shower in the school shower rooms, had clutched her hands to her ears and over her head, screaming the water mustn't touch her head. So after that, dimly, dimly, she sensed it, she was different and they knew her difference and kept away. There was talk that her father and mother were taking her back to Earth next year; it seemed vital to her that they do so, though it would mean the loss of thousands of dollars to her family. And so, the children hated her for all these reasons of big and little consequence. They hated her pale snow face, her waiting silence, her thinness, and her possible future.

ISBN 9780170195928

1 A **noun** is a naming word. There are four main types of nouns: common, proper, collective and abstract.
   - Highlight an example of five common nouns.
   - Highlight an example of a proper noun.
   - Highlight an example of an abstract noun.

2 The **pronoun** takes the place of a noun. List the pronouns used in this extract. _____

3 **Adjectives** describe nouns and pronouns. They are often called describing words. List the adjectives used in this extract. _____

4 A **verb** is a 'doing' or an 'action' word. List the verbs used in this extract.

5 **Adverbs** are words that tell us more about verbs. They give us more information about how, when, or where something is done. Can you find an example of an adverb in the extract above?

6 **Conjunctions** are connecting words that join two or more sentences into a single sentence. List the conjunctions used in this extract. _____

7 **Prepositions** are the 'small words' that usually relate two words or groups of words to one another. List the prepositions used in this extract. _____

Group 2: Punctuation

Punctuation marks make the written text easier to read and understand.
Without punctuation, writing would not make sense.

Capital letters

1 **Sentences always start with capital letters.**
2 **Proper nouns need a capital letter.**
3 **The main words in titles of books, films, plays, songs and so on are written using capital letters.**

Correct the following sentences using **capital letters** where appropriate.
1 we visited napier in the school holidays.
2 doctor barrett explained that it was necessary for me to have a blood test.
3 yesterday my mum took me to pak'nsave to buy the ingredients for my birthday dinner.
4 my younger brother, jack, is a pain in the neck!
5 sir peter blake is an inspiration to all new zealanders.
6 our prime minister will visit waitangi on the 6th of february.

Full stop

The full stop (.) shows the reader when one sentence (one idea) is complete.

Correct the following sentences using **capital letters** and **full stops** where appropriate.
1 i have decided to take drama, geography and graphics next year
2 megan was the best ballet dancer i knew she was incredibly light on her feet
3 i am in year 9 and go to whangarei girls' high school i am in the junior touch rugby team
4 my favourite book is 'to kill a mockingbird' by harper lee i had to read it in english last year
5 tomorrow is our last game of soccer for the season i am not going to miss getting up early on a saturday morning

Question mark

The question mark is a sign that a question has been asked.

Exclamation mark

The exclamation mark is a sign that shows strong emotion, or when somebody is shouting.

Correct the following sentences by placing a **full stop, exclamation or question mark** where appropriate.
1 I am the baby of the family
2 I am so scared
3 Why do we need an education
4 For goodness sake would you hurry up
5 Where are you going
6 What will happen next
7 It is important that you arrive on time
8 Do we have to go Mum it is soooo boring
9 We have been in the car a long time how much further to go
10 Ouch That really hurt

ISBN 9780170195928

The comma

The comma shows links in a sentence as well as separating items within a sentence.

Each sentence needs one or two **commas**. Put them in the correct place(s).

1　I left the house at six hoping to reach the sports ground before seven o'clock.
2　Sue went to the shop to buy candles balloons and streamers for the party.
3　My mother's favourite band Split Enz is on the TV tonight.
4　After playing rugby in the morning he went to play soccer in the afternoon.
5　Chess is a fascinating game more challenging than draughts.
6　My brother who is the hungriest person in the world just loves pizza.

Apostrophe

Apostrophes can be used to show contractions or possession.

Write out the **contraction** for the following phrases in the space provided.

1　would have _____
2　does not _____
3　they are _____
4　do not _____
5　they will _____
6　have not _____

Decide whether each sentence uses the **apostrophe** in the correct place or not.
If it does, write T (True); if not, write F (False).

1　He's the fastest runner in the school.
2　Im going to the movies' tonight.
3　Where's the cheese?
4　He is very sick and shouldnt be going to school today.
5　Cant I have some more pocket money, Mum?
6　The waka was put back in its resting place after the traditional welcome.
7　Weve been to the beach today.
8　The team owes its win to the goalkeeper's skill.

Inverted commas/speech marks

Inverted commas/speech marks are used at the beginning and end of groups of words that are actually *spoken*.

Decide whether each sentence uses **speech marks** in the correct place or not.
If it does, write T (True); if not, write F (False).

1　Miss Price said, 'There will be no homework over this weekend.'
2　'Could you pass the sugar please, Ben'?
3　Martin Luther King said, 'I have a dream!'
4　Rebecca leapt up. 'What do you think you are doing?' 'You should be at school!'
5　A voice came over the airport speaker system. Would Karen O'Reilly please make her way to the gate.

Let's recap word classes

Use a blue pen to punctuate the following extract from the Ray Bradbury short story *All Summer in a Day*. (We've left a bit of it there to help you out.)

now dont go too far called the teacher after them youve only two hours you know You wouldnt want to get caught out

But they were running and turning their faces up to the sky and feeling the sun on their cheeks like a warm iron they were taking off their jackets and letting the sun burn their arms

oh, its better than the sun lamps isn't it

much, much better

they stopped running and stood in the great jungle that covered Venus, that grew and never stopped growing, tumultuously, even as you watched it

Check it

A sentence is a group of words that together express a complete thought.

Select to which **sentence type** these sentences belong. Choose from either *simple*, *compound* or *complex*.

1 Golf is a great game. _____

2 Get some milk and top up the petrol, please. _____

3 She cut my hair but I didn't like it. _____

4 Ancient Egyptians had good dentists. _____

5 This coffee is strong because I ordered an espresso. _____

Select to which **sentence type** this sentence belongs. Choose from either *imperative sentence*, *exclamatory sentence*, *minor sentence* or *rhetorical question*.

1 Leave me alone, please. _____

2 It's a goal! _____

3 Very tasty, thanks. _____

4 Do you think I'm an idiot? _____

5 Is she for real? _____

6 Take the next road on the right. _____

7 Fantastic! _____

Let's recap syntax

In this extract from the short story *All Summer in a Day* three sentences have been highlighted in bold. They are a minor sentence, a compound sentence and a simple sentence. Which is which?

> 'Ready?'
> 'Ready.'
> 'Now?
> **'Soon.'**
> 'Do the scientists really know? Will it happen today, will it?'
> 'Look, look; see for yourself !'
> The children pressed to each other like so many roses, so many weeds, intermixed, peering out for a look at the hidden sun.
> **It rained.**
> It had been raining for seven years; thousands upon thousands of days compounded and filled from one end to the other with rain, with the drum and gush of water, with the sweet crystal fall of showers and the concussion of storms so heavy they were tidal waves come over the islands. **A thousand forests had been crushed under the rain and grown up a thousand times to be crushed again.** And this was the way life was forever on the planet Venus, and this was the schoolroom of the children of the rocket men and women who had come to a raining world to set up civilization and live out their lives.
> 'It's stopping, it's stopping!'
> 'Yes, yes!'

Group 4: Figures of speech

The simile

A simile is a direct comparison that always contains the words 'as' or 'like'.

Decide whether the following sentences include a **simile** or not by writing T (True) or F (False) in each box.

1 The baby was like a pig when it ate. ☐

2 The house was as solid as a rock. ☐

3 He's a solid kind of person. ☐

ISBN 9780170195928

4 The house is built on solid rock.

5 She danced as delicately as a butterfly.

6 That's a piggy way of eating.

7 Excitement swelled up inside them.

8 The burglar moved with cat-like stealth through the garden.

The metaphor

A metaphor is a comparison which does not use 'like' or 'as'.

Decide whether the following sentences include a **metaphor** or not by writing T (True) or F (False) in each box.

1 He is like a pig when he eats.

2 He is a pig when he eats.

3 The soldiers were herded into the cave.

4 The young girl sang like a nightingale.

5 'You're a wise owl,' said the teacher to his student.

6 The farmer ploughed his paddock.

7 The ship ploughed through the waves.

Identify the metaphor in the following sentences by either underlining or highlighting the phrase.

8 The bedclothes were hills on her unmade bed.

9 The thief was a silent shadow lurking in the darkest corners.

10 A silver ball hung in the night sky.

11 Her anger was a searing, hot blast through the whole room.

12 The heavy rain was a drum.

Personification

Personification is where a non-living object is given living qualities, writing of it as if it were a living person.

Decide whether the following sentences include a **personification** or not by writing T (True) or F (False) in each box.

1 The wind was attacking the flowers.

2 The trees sighed happily in the breeze.

3 As the sun set like a huge apricot, George walked the trail.

4 The waves were large animals looming above him.

5 Bored blowflies whine monotonously in the still air.

6 The colourful flowers shimmered like exquisite lace in the summer breeze.

7 The butterflies flitted joyfully around the beautiful garden.

8 The moss was a green cloak enveloping the big rock.

9 The creeping shadows lurked in the dark corners.

10 The clouds were soft and wispy like feathers.

Alliteration

Alliteration is the repetition of consonant sounds at the beginning of words placed closely together to create a sound echo.

Decide whether the following phrases use **alliteration** or not by writing T (True) or F (False) in each box.

1 Friend or foe!

2 law and order

3 criminal conspiracy

4 Fish – the family dish.

5 pickled peppers

6 sound spectacular

7 Windy Wellington

Getting tricky!

8 friendly photographer

9 the circling cat

10 the capable citizen

11 The knight felt nauseous.

ISBN 9780170195928

Identify the **alliteration** in the following sentences by either underlining or highlighting the repeated consonant sound.

1 He ran to the rocks.
2 The rabbits rushed raucously around their hutch.
3 The cat silently stalked its unsuspecting prey.
4 The snow drifted like leaves onto the lawn.
5 The stream rambled and burbled breathlessly through the field.
6 The snake slipped and slithered menacingly through the field.
7 The photographer flashed and filmed effusively.
8 The butcher's face became red and ruddy, carrying the heavy rump and rissoles.

Assonance

Assonance is the repetition of vowel sounds. The trick is not to think of it as the same *letter*, but the same *sound*.

Decide whether the following sentences include **assonance** or not by writing T (True) or F (False) in each box.

1 He heard a dull, pulsating sound.

2 A large crack ripped through the night and woke Nathan.

3 She gazed at a sea of green.

4 'What was that?' he said, as he sat bolt upright in bed.

5 His thin limbs were delicate.

6 The only sound now was the buzzing of a large blowfly butting up against the window, behind which a street lamp glowed.

7 They walked down the wind-dried road.

8 The wind sighed through the trees.

9 I stood upon the shore.

10 Troubles rested on my shoulders.

Onomatopoeia

Onomatopoeia uses words that imitate and reproduce real-life sounds and actions.

Decide whether the following sentences include **onomatopoeia** or not by writing T (True) or F (False) in each box.

1 We could hear the stormy sea booming through the caves.

2 The supermarket trolley went careering noisily down the aisle.

3 We heard huge clangs when the church bell was rung.

4 The boy leapt into the pool with a huge displacement of water.

5 We could hear the crunch of their footsteps when they walked along the stony path.

6 The waves landed heavily on the beach at the height of the storm.

Rhyme

Rhyme is the repetition of final vowel and consonant sounds in words. Two types of rhyme you may see at this level are full and internal.

Decide whether the following sentences include **rhyme** or not by writing T (True) or F (False) in each box.

1 The wind-dried road stretched far into the distance.

2 You do the crime, you do the time.

3 A dull, pulsating sound was heard.

4 The rain in Spain falls mainly on the plain.

5 His thin limbs were delicate.

6 Do not conceal thy radiant eye
The starlight of serenest skies

7 The fair breeze blew, the white foam flew,
The furrow followed free

ISBN 9780170195928

8   I watch him striding lank behind
    His clashing team.

9   Wee Willie Winkie ran through the town
    Upstairs and downstairs in his nightgown.

10 It cracked and growled, and roared and howled.

Rhythm

Rhythm is a particular pattern that suggests movement or pace.

1   Learn the following verse from Jack Prelutsky's poem *The Witch*. Listen to the rhythm. Note especially how the last line has to be said slowly and this is to emphasise the witch's wickedness.

> She comes by night, in fearsome flight,
> in garments black as pitch,
> the queen of doom upon her broom,
> the wild and wicked witch.

2   Learn the following verse from *The Highwayman*. Listen to the rhythm. Note especially the regular sound of the galloping horse.

> The wind was a torrent of darkness among the gusty trees,
> The moon was a ghostly galleon tossed upon cloudy seas,
> The road was a ribbon of moonlight, over the purple moor,
> And the highwayman came riding –
> Riding – riding –
> The highwayman came riding, up to the old inn-door.

Let's recap figures of speech

Read the extract from the Ray Bradbury short story *All Summer in a Day* below. Then write one example of each of the identified poetic terms.

Margot stood apart from them, from these children who could never remember a time when there wasn't rain and rain and rain. They were all nine years old, and if there had been a day, seven years ago, when the sun came out for an hour and showed its face to the stunned world, they could not recall. Sometimes, at night, she heard them stir, in remembrance, and she knew they were dreaming and remembering gold or a yellow crayon or a coin large enough to buy the world with. She knew they thought they remembered a warmness, like a blushing in the face, in the body, in the arms and legs and trembling hands. But then they always awoke to the tatting drum, the endless shaking down of clear bead necklaces upon the roof, the walk, the gardens, the forests, and their dreams were gone.

All day yesterday they had read in class about the sun. About how like a lemon it was, and how hot. And they had written small stories or essays or poems about it:

I think the sun is a flower,
That blooms for just one hour.

That was Margot's poem, read in a quiet voice in the still classroom while the rain was falling outside.

'Aw, you didn't write that!' protested one of the boys.

'I did,' said Margot. 'I did.'

'William!' said the teacher.

But that was yesterday. Now the rain was slackening, and the children were crushed in the great thick windows.

'Where's teacher?'

'She'll be back.'

'She'd better hurry, we'll miss it!'

They turned on themselves, like a feverish wheel, all tumbling spokes. Margot stood alone.

1   Simile   _____

2   Metaphor   _____

3   Personification   _____

4   Alliteration   _____

5   Onomatopoeia   _____

ISBN 9780170195928

Storyboard

Use the storyboard below to complete the activity on pages 128–130 of *How to ... Achieve in Year 9 English*.

Shot No.		Shot Type:
		Dialogue/Soundtrack:

Shot No.		Shot Type:
		Dialogue/Soundtrack:

Shot No.		Shot Type:
		Dialogue/Soundtrack:

Shot No.		Shot Type:
		Dialogue/Soundtrack:

Shot No.		Shot Type:
		Dialogue/Soundtrack:

Shot No.		Shot Type:
		Dialogue/Soundtrack:

ISBN 9780170195928

Shot No.		Shot Type:
		Dialogue/Soundtrack:

Shot No.		Shot Type:
		Dialogue/Soundtrack.

Shot No.		Shot Type:
		Dialogue/Soundtrack:

Shot No.		Shot Type:
		Dialogue/Soundtrack:

Shot No.		Shot Type:
		Dialogue/Soundtrack:

Shot No.		Shot Type:
		Dialogue/Soundtrack:

ISBN 9780170195928

13

Looking at speechwriting

This activity connects to page 140 of *How to ... Achieve in Year 9 English*.

It is useful to look at the structure of someone else's work before you begin writing your own speech. Annotate the speech where it demonstrates use of:

- personal pronouns
- statistics
- metaphor
- rhetorical questions
- bridging words and phrases
- ironic humour
- links to its audience
- links between introduction and conclusion
- where voice intonation, gesture and eye contact might be particularly effective.

Let me tell you about something I've been doing for almost 13 years now, something which has, in fact, been a significant focus of virtually my entire life up to this point. It's an endeavour that is almost finished; a long journey that has all but reached its destination. What is it that I've been doing for so long and with such commitment and dedication?

Preparing to become a TEENAGER!

As I've already mentioned, I've put a lot of time and effort into this project. In recent months I've been doing some serious research into the facts, figures and statistics of teenage-hood, putting the finishing touches to my 13 year preparation to enter this new phase in my life. After all, I want to be as well prepared as I can be for turning 13.

I've discovered that the word "teenager" only began to be used after World War Two. I consider myself very fortunate to live in an age when I can actually be a teenager! Just imagine ... If I'd lived 70 years ago, I'd be about to become a "youth"! Doesn't sound nearly as much fun, does it?

What other important, eye-opening information have I discovered in my research?

Well, I've found that New Zealand teenagers are more likely than other groups to live in urban areas rather than rural communities. And that the main cause of teenage death in our country is road accidents. That's sad, but sadder still is the fact that the second main cause of death is suicide.

Another thing I've found is that 8% of New Zealand teenagers have a disability which limits their daily activity, and that 6% of teenagers do some vigorous physical activity at least once a week.

ISBN 9780170195928

These sorts of facts are interesting, and help me get an overview of teenage life in New Zealand, but facts and information alone will not make me a success at being a teenager. There are numerous important skills I need to learn, and areas in which I need to develop, and it's these things I've been working on so hard for so long. I have been extremely fortunate to grow up with an older brother and sister who have provided me with expert, full-time, on-the-job training in the intricacies of teenage living; they've put me through rigorous courses in such important matters as teenage bedroom care.

I'm embarrassed to admit it, but by nature I'm a very tidy person ... and of course that would just never do for a fully-fledged teenager. I used to always keep my bedroom in an immaculate condition and if such behaviour were to continue into my teenage years, naturally it would result in my immediate expulsion from the teenagers' union! I have had an expert in my brother to help me overcome this problem, and I've really been working hard at becoming sufficiently messy to qualify for teenage-hood. Certainly my mother has noticed the difference, which is very gratifying! My brother has been a wonderful role model for me in this area, and although I can't yet get close to the level of untidiness that he maintains in his bedroom, seemingly without any effort at all, I really am improving my ability at keeping my room in a shambles 24/7! I'm hoping eventually to be able to pass on my skills to my two younger sisters, and be the sort of example for them that my brother has been for me. After all, isn't that what families are for?

Another crucial area I've been working on is my intellectual development. As everyone knows, the major task of any self-respecting teenager is to educate their parents. Parents of teenagers seem to have a special knack of saying and doing foolish things, which completely embarrass their children! Part of a teenager's job description is to know everything, so you can try and educate your parents and make them at least passably sensible! So I've been working very hard to build up my knowledge pool, and am pleased to say that I now know just about everything, and am almost ready to begin my parents' re-training.

The countdown has now begun. Only four days to go until I become a teenager. And I think I'm just about all set! It's been a long period of preparation, but I've covered all the bases and I'm feeling pretty confident that I'll be a natural!!

ISBN 9780170195928

HINT FOR SUCCESS
Write so that your words can be read easily – clear handwriting is a very important skill.

Focus 1: Understanding poetry

Read this poem several times before you begin.

The Boxer

Metaphor

The great iron figure crouches,
Scabs like flowers on his knees,   Simile _____
And his chest is like a mountain
And his legs are thick as trees.

Simile _____   Simile _____

He spits blood like a cherub
In a fountain spouting foam,
Ringed around by swimming ropes
And punters going home.

Broken-knuckled, shiny-eyed.
Battered, bruised, and wet
With droplets like cold rubies,   Alliteration
And laced with bitter sweat.

Alliteration

He crouches in a corner
In his pool of sparkling red
And dreads the jeers which soon will fall
Like blows upon his head.

                              Simile _____

By Emma Payne

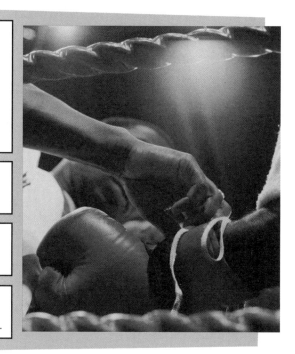

Similes
Annotate the highlighted simile that best describes each of the following features of the boxer.
A   He has a previous knee injury.
B   He has lost the fight.
C   He has been injured in the fight.
D   He has worked out and trained.

Metaphor
Draw a line linking the metaphor box to the metaphor in the poem.

Alliteration
Draw a line linking each alliteration box to a different example.

Rhyme
Use a red pen to underline the pairs of rhyming words in each verse.

ISBN 9780170195928

You will hear your teacher talking about 'imagery'. Imagery in writing is descriptive language that usually appeals to the senses. The images may be formed by literal description or by figures of speech such as similes and metaphors.

When you look in a mirror, you see an image – a likeness of yourself. When you use a camera and take a picture of your friend, the photograph is an image of that person. If you write a description of your friend, you are creating an image of that person in words. In writing, an image is a picture made up from words.

One of the most commonly used figures of speech is the simile. Similes are comparisons that use the words 'like' or 'as' to point out the comparison. For example, 'The pale moon gleamed in a dark sky, round as a white plate on a dark tablecloth.' Here you are asked to imagine the cold, white china of the plate and the dark, dense fabric of the cloth and then think more clearly of this particular moon in this particular sky.

Metaphors are also comparisons, which suggest one part of the comparison has some of the qualities of the other part. For example, 'My dad has sandpaper hands.' You know Dad's hands aren't really made of sandpaper but you can easily imagine his rough skin, can't you?

You do:

Imagery is used in both poetry and in prose writing. You choose your own way: write either a poem or a passage of descriptive writing.

Take a weather situation: imagine the weather is a person (old, young, angry, sad, serious, joker, male, female etc) and write about what it is trying to do to people, or the land, or the earth. Use your own experience of a weather situation to help you imagine what you want your reader to 'see'. Remember how simile and metaphor can help to create the image.

Here are some suggestions:

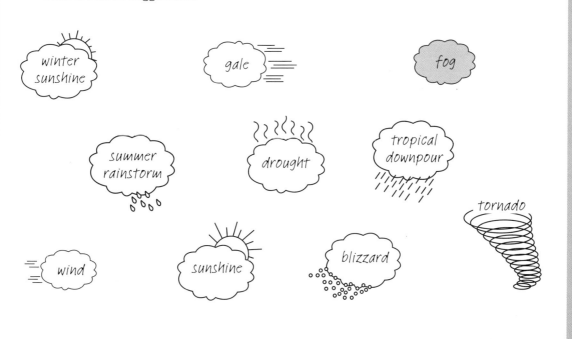

ISBN 9780170195928

Week _____ Date for completion _____

Parent's sig. _____ Teacher's sig. _____

Focus 1: Creative writing

So how do you tackle creative writing?

The process of writing does not change whether you have one hour or one week!

Just remember:

To help you get started we have suggested a process below.

1 Look over the starters given. It is likely one or two will grab your attention. Look closely at this again and decide which gives you the most scope to work with.

2 Plan the story by brainstorming all your ideas.
   - Are you going to write a descriptive or narrative piece?
   - Be sure you have a beginning, middle and end.
   - Think about your characters and how they will speak.

3 Write your piece, remembering to stick to the plan. A well-planned piece of writing will take you much less time to write than an unplanned piece.

4 Now leave your piece of writing. Come back to it at a later time and then …

5 Reread your piece of writing.

6 Edit your piece. Check your:
   - Spelling
   - Vocabulary
   - Sentence structure: Can you make it more interesting? Vary it?
   - Opening
   - Closing.

7 Write the final copy of your story in the back of this book. Don't forget to check over your work once you have finished or get someone else to read it through. It is easy to miss little mistakes!

Starters

Choose one of the following starters to begin your work. Aim to write at least 200 words.

1 People swarmed onto the intersection as the crossing buzzer shrilled …

2 The crowd watched with anticipation …

3 Then it was Monday. In the space of a weekend the world had changed …

4 Seventeen steps …

5 I often felt left out …

6 It was just my luck …

Here are some clues to help you understand what the markers do not want to see.

- A piece of writing that is not very interesting.
- A piece of writing that is all one paragraph.
- A piece of writing that is too short.
- A lot of errors in grammar, punctuation and spelling.

Here are some clues to help you understand what your teacher is looking for.

- An original story that shows planning and thought.
- A piece of writing that shows you knew the end of the story before you began.
- A variety of vocabulary.
- Clear paragraphing.

ISBN 9780170195928

Prefixes

A prefix is a group of letters that is added to the front of a root word and changes its meaning.

Prefixes may create new words: **im**migrate   **pre**occupied
Prefixes may create antonyms: **un**friendly   **dis**satisfied

Don't worry if there is a 'double up' of letters when you join a prefix and root word together. In most cases neither the prefix nor the root word changes when you join them together.

For example: u**n** + **n**ecessary = u**nn**ecessary

You do:

Add a prefix to the underlined word to make the sentence make sense.

1   Move in an _____clockwise direction

2   The painter put a dog in the _____ground of his painting.

3   The _____employment figures grew in the recession.

4   The principal _____approved of the student's mohawk hairstyle.

5   The winner of American Idol became a _____star overnight.

Suffixes

A suffix is a group of letters that is added to the end of a root word and changes its meaning.

Here are a few examples of suffixes; all of them begin with a vowel:

able   al   ed   en   er   est   et   ing   ish   ist   ous   ive

When a word has one vowel before a single final consonant, double that consonant before adding the suffix.
For example: shop   shopp**ed**   shopp**ing**   shopp**er**
                   clap   clapp**ed**   clapp**ing**   clapp**er**

When the word ends in a silent e (which makes the vowel inside the word long), then drop that e before adding the ending.
For example: skate   skat**ed**   skat**ing**   skat**er**
                   arrive   arriv**ed**   arriv**ing**   arriv**al**

You do:

In the following sentences add a suffix to the underlined word to fill the space in the sentence.

1   I like John; he's a _____ person.

2   Write clearly if you want to be a good _____ .

3   This plum is ripe but that plum is _____ .

4   Go to the shop and collect my _____ , please.

5   There is danger here. This place is _____ .

19

ISBN 9780170195928

Week _____ Date for completion _____

Parent's sig. _____ Teacher's sig. _____

Focus 1: Your school library

Draw the layout of your school library in the space below. Mark the following on your diagram:

Fiction	Non-fiction	Reference	Computers	Vertical File
Photocopier	Study desks	Casual seating	The librarian's office	Issues counter

Magazine and newspaper racks

ISBN 9780170195928

	Answer	Term
a		**Reference book**
b		**Index**
c		**Encyclopedia**
d		**Catalogue**
e		**Fiction**
f		**Non-fiction**
g		**Dewey Decimal System**
h		**Due date**
i		**Author**

	Answer	Term
j		**Non-print**
k		**Keyword**
l		**Table of contents**
m		**Yearbook**
n		**Genre**
o		**Internet**
p		**Desk copy**
q		**Anthology**

1   Novels, short stories, reading for pleasure.

2   A word indicating a main term or concept or subject discussed in a document; used in searching catalogues.

3   Books about facts – everything from A to Z.

4   Records, with detailed descriptions and location information, of the materials in a library collection. In most libraries it is stored on a computer.

5   An alphabetical detailed list of the names, places and subjects discussed in a book and the numbers of the pages on which each subject is treated. Usually found at the back of the book.

6   A list of the chapter or article titles in a book or journal. This is usually found at the beginning of a book after the title page.

7   A book such as a dictionary, encyclopedia or directory, which contains specific facts, data or other brief bits of information. It may not be borrowed.

8   An annual documentary, historical or memorial publication containing information about the previous year.

9   A library search term used to find examples of a type of literature, for example fantasy, mystery.

10   A reference book containing information on all subjects, or limited to a special field or subject. Sometimes in more than one volume.

11   A global network connecting millions of computers. This includes but is not limited to the World Wide Web. It can be used for e-mail and other functions.

12   The date by which borrowed materials must be returned to the library or renewed.

13   Books that are held by the librarians due to them being in high demand by students. Access is only allowed on a period-by-period basis.

14   A writer of a book, essay, story, play, poem or other work.

15   Materials published in a format other than print on paper, for example audio/video cassettes, CD-ROMs, DVDs.

16   A collection of poems, short stories or essays, by more than one author.

17   A system of classifying books and other materials by subject using a numerical system so that like materials are shelved next to each other.

ISBN 9780170195928

UNIT 4

Week _____ Date for completion _____

Parent's sig. _____ Teacher's sig. _____

Focus 1: Theme essay

This activity asks you to write a clear, detailed, thoughtful essay. Complete the information in the box below before you begin.

Title of text: _____   Author of text: _____

Let's recap how to write a literary essay

By now you will be aware of the basic structure you can use to write your essay.

Don't forget to use quotations to support your ideas. Go to page 98 of your *How to …* textbook to remind yourself on how to best incorporate quotations in your essay.

> **Introduction**
> This paragraph should always:
> - give the title and author (director, poet) of the text
> - give the genre (novel, short story, poem, film)
> - refer to the question.
>
> **Body paragraphs**
> The body of the essay is divided into paragraphs. How many will depend on the type of question you're asked. Generally a body paragraph should have:
> - a topic sentence that clearly states what the paragraph will be about
> - detail from the text
> - relevant quotations
> - explanation
> - a sentence to link back to the original idea.
>
> **Conclusion**
> This will include:
> - no new information (it shows a lack of prior planning)
> - a restatement of the main point of your essay, strongly referring back to the question.

Let's have a look at the essay topic you have been given.

> ### Describe an idea that interested you in the text. Explain why it interested you.

Using a red or blue pen, annotate the question with the following.
- Put brackets around each part of the question.
- Underline the key words in the question.

In this box decide upon the following things.
- List the possible themes you could use for this topic.
- For each theme brainstorm at least two reasons why it was interesting.
- Think about some of the following things: Is it relevant to you? Could you apply it to something you are going through? Is it topical to other people your age?

Theme	Reasons
1	1
	2
2	1
	2
3	1
	2

ISBN 9780170195928

Evaluate the information you have in your box (page 22). Hopefully one idea/theme stands out as being easier to write about than the others.

- Look through your idea/theme handouts/notes.
- Go back to the key places in the text and reread them. Take notes and copy suitable quotes.
- Use a different-colour pen to group and structure your information.

You should now be ready to begin writing your essay. Use your own refill to draft your work. Write the final copy of your essay in the back of this book.

Focus 2: Clichés

Clichés are expressions that have been used so often that they have lost their original effect. Phrases that have now become clichés often began as interesting and distinctive expressions, but, after being used over and over again, all their sparkle and originality have disappeared.

Take a look at the following expressions that have become clichés over the years.

For instance look at the expression 'The fledglings have left the nest.' The literal meaning for this is that the small birds have left their nest, that is, they have grown up and flown away. The figurative meaning of this is that the children have grown up and left home.

Give the figurative meaning of each of the following expressions.

A bolt from the blue

To move the goal posts

To beat around the bush

Under a cloud

Under the weather

English is full of these sorts of expressions. See how many you can think of or look up some that have the word 'cat' in them. There are at least 15!

You might find your parents useful when doing the tasks in this Focus!

ISBN 9780170195928

Focus 1: Written close reading

By now you will have done some work honing your close reading skills. We assume you have worked through the exercises in the *How to …* textbook.

Helpful hints	
There are a few things we recommend you do before you attempt a passage:	1 Read the text carefully.
	2 Read the questions.
	3 Read the text again.
	4 Work through the questions one at a time.

Ancient rituals usher in New Year

For the substantial Chinese community on the Shore, the Spring Festival, more commonly known as Chinese New Year, is the most important festival in the Chinese lunar calendar. ERROL KIONG reports on some practices associated with the lunar new year, and how the Shore's Chinese community are ushering in the Year of the Black Sheep tomorrow.

The Chinese sleep early on the fourth day of Chinese New Year so the mice can get married.

The mice have free run of the house for one night of the year, procreating, feasting and generally causing havoc, in the hope that they won't finish the house owner's rice stocks, says Chinese affairs commentator Terry Teng.

This is just one of the many observances of Chinese New Year, which falls on February 1.

It is the most important event in the Chinese lunar calendar and, like its Western equivalent, has many traditions and rituals.

Its origin is centuries old, too old to be traced. Also known as the Spring Festival, Chinese New Year ushers in the start of spring in China, with celebrations lasting 15 days.

Preparations tend to begin a month before when people start buying presents, decoration materials, food and clothing.

A frenzy of cleaning also ensues days before the New Year, when Chinese houses are cleaned from top to

GOOD TIDINGS: *A Chinese spring scroll bearing congratulations for the new year.*

bottom to sweep away the bad luck of the previous year.

Doors and windows are given a new coat of paint, usually in red, an auspicious colour signifying wealth and luck.

Red scrolls bearing traditional themes of happiness, prosperity and peace for the coming year are then placed on doors and windows on New Year's Eve.

He still observes many of the more obscure rituals of the spring festival. The columnist for Auckland's Chinese-language newspapers and author of six books about New Zealand, feels it's important to keep traditions alive.

One New Year tradition is to not sweep or clean the house during the first five days, as it signifies sweeping luck out the door. Mr Teng says rubbish must be swept behind the door and kept there until after the fifth day.

In fact, no cooking and cleaning is to be done, only eating, drinking and having fun, says Mr Teng.

On the surface

1 What is the Chinese New Year also known as? _____

2 Why are Chinese homes cleaned thoroughly before New Year? _____

_____

3 Which colour is given special significance during the New Year season? _____

_____

ISBN 9780170195928

4 How long do the celebrations for Chinese New Year last? _____

5 Name one special tradition are observed during Chinese New Year? _____
_____

Technical

6 Explain clearly why Mr Teng has been interviewed as part of this article. _____
_____

7 Why do you think the journalist began his article explaining a tradition involving mice?
_____
_____

Search and think

8 Which two paragraphs does the photo best match? Why?
_____

Focus 2: Apostrophes

The poor apostrophe is probably the most misused punctuation mark – either it isn't there when it's needed or it's put into places where it doesn't belong. There are examples everywhere you look. Here's a greengrocer who just can't get it right!

Remember – an apostrophe is used in two main ways:

- **Contraction** – one or more letters has or have been missed out.

  For example, 'isn't' means 'is not' – the 'o' has been dropped.

- **Possession** – something belongs to something else.

  For example, the dog's tail – the dog owns, or possesses, the tail.

Its spring — come in and buy spring vegetables today!
(It's (It is) spring, he means)

Carrot's on special
(just one carrot, then?)

New potato's and kumara
(one potato's what???)

Get you're gourmet greens here
(Get you are greens...?)

Only 'its' seems to cause problems for students. Just remember, if you can use 'it is' or 'it has' instead, then an apostrophe is required. For example:

It's a long way to the beach. Even the dog will need to take its lunch along.

You do:

1 As this is a bit of an issue, here's an exercise for you to test yourself. Read this short passage and put in all the necessary apostrophes. Use a bright felt pen and only put one in when you *know* it is needed.

Susan stood at the edge of the lake watching the windsurfers. Ill never be able to do that she thought to herself.

'Dad, I dont want to do this,' she said to her father, standing beside her.

'Im sure youll be fine once you get started,' he reassured her, 'its easy, really it is.'

One windsurfers sail suddenly keeled over and he slipped off his board into the murky water. Watching him claw his way back to the boards surface with great difficulty, Susan sighed and picked up her sisters wetsuit. Better get it over with, Dad wasnt going to give up that easily.

ISBN 9780170195928

Focus 1: Visual close reading – look and see

image (superimposed) point of contrast

logos/points of contrast

ROCKET FUEL FOR YOUR CAREER!

Careers in retail rock! If you don't want to be stuck behind a desk all day in a boring office environment doing the same thing over and over again... choose retail for a future that's going places. Why retail?

Retail offers career paths, fast progression and promotion and great job opportunities.

Retail has variety – positions include Visual Merchandiser, Buyer, Account Manager, Regional Manager, Marketing Manager, Financial Controller, Managing Director and loads more.

Retail is fun! Fast-paced, funky products, cool colleagues, wicked high-energy atmosphere and great money!

NZQA qualifications available nationwide while working full-time and getting full-pay. No exams, no fees and no student loan! Go to www.retailito.org.nz for information on retail qualifications.

WHY RETAIL?
WHY NOT!
www.rwr.co.nz

tone = _____

There is space to label each of these techniques on the advertisement. Fill in the gaps.

Layout
- Headline
- Image
- Body copy
- Background
- Logo/slogan

Visual techniques
Point of contrast
Bold lettering
Logos

Verbal techniques
Tone of language
Play on words
Repetition
Use of adjectives for effect
Personal pronouns
Alliteration
Rhetorical question
Contractions

ISBN 9780170195928

Now you have spent some time analysing the advertisement, answer the questions that follow.

1 a   Who/what is being advertised (product/service)?'

   _____

   b   Who is being targeted (audience)?

   _____

   c   What is the overall message we are intended to get from the text (message)?

   _____

2   Clearly explain the connection between the background graphic and the rest of the advertisement.

   _____

   _____

   _____

   _____

   _____

   _____

3   How does the language of this article aim to reach the teenage market? Use examples from the text in your
     answer.

   _____

   _____

   _____

   _____

   _____

4   Why is the word 'retail' used so many times?

   _____

5   What is the significance of the logos on the right-hand side of the advertisement?

   _____

   _____

   _____

6   Why have most of these logos been put on a plain white background?

   _____

   _____

7   At the bottom of the advertisement you are given a website, www.rwr.co.nz. Look carefully through the rest of the
     advertisement to find out what the 'rwr' stands for.

   _____

   _____

27

Focus 1: Understanding poetry

Do you remember the process to analysing a poem?

Step 1: Read – preferably aloud.

Step 2: Reread quietly.

Step 3: Use dictionary to help you with difficult vocabulary.

Step 4: Read again.

Step 5: Discuss as a class/in pairs.

Step 6: Reread the poem. Enjoy it!

Step 8: Answer any questions that follow.

Look up the highlighted words. Use the arrows to help you with your annotation.
- tethered
- senescent
- sodden
- shackled
- recast
- galley
- surly

The following techniques have been underlines for you. Annotate them in the space provided.
- Personification
- Alliteration
- Onomatopoeia
- Repetition
- Metaphor

NB: If you get stuck, you might want to do the activity at the bottom of page 29 first.

Dinghy at the Water's Edge

Tethered at the salt water's edge
This senescent hull has nowhere now
To go. All that's left of her
Is a bared wooden keel; the rotted floor

Is back with the sea. Each day
The sliding tide laps up to lick
And lick again long sodden remains,
And whispering, returns to the belly

Of the harbour. Each night the same.
A fisherman I watched used once
To row her out. No longer though, for
She lies shackled on soft mangrove mud.

When boys see her they slosh to her
There. Boarding, they recast her to sea
In their game. She is a galley and they
Surly sea men guiding her knowingly to shore.

by John Geraets

ISBN 9780170195928

Answer the following questions:

1 Using words/phrases from the poem, describe the dinghy in the poem.

_____

_____

_____

2 To what features of the sea is the poet alluding with the lines
   'The sliding tide laps up to lick / and lick again ...'?

_____

_____

_____

3 How do you know that the poet has watched this dinghy for many years?

_____

_____

_____

_____

4 In the last stanza the poet uses the word 'game'. What is the game and who is playing it?

_____

_____

_____

_____

Focus 2: Poetry recap

Time to put your thinking caps on. Match the terms, definitions and examples below using the grid to record your answers.

Term	Definition	Example
1 ALLITERATION	(a) When a word, line or verse is repeated several times in the poem.	(i) Her eyes shone like diamonds.
2 METAPHOR	(b) When the word that is being used sounds like the action it is describing.	(ii) Silly Sally sat sadly upon the satin sheets.
3 SIMILE	(c) Giving a non-human object human characteristics.	(iii) The sea moaned, moaned, moaned.
4 REPETITION	(d) Saying that something *is* something else.	(iv) And all the trees have silver skirts.
5 ONOMATOPOEIA	(e) Saying something is like something else – always use 'like' or 'as'.	(v) I've got a dog as thin as a rail, He's got fleas all over his tail.
6 RHYME	(f) The repetition of sounds at the beginning of a group of words.	(vi) The wind was a whip that cracked over our heads.
7 PERSONIFICATION	(g) When the ends of the words sound the same.	(vii) We cursed the horrible six-inch sludge!

Term	1	2	3	4	5	6	7
Definition							
Example							

ISBN 9780170195928

Week _____ Date for completion _____

Parent's sig. _____ Teacher's sig. _____

Focus 1: Formal writing – how to plan

You do:

Your task is to plan a formal essay on the topic:

> **Wind energy is the way of the future.**

Begin with what you know about this topic.

To complete this task effectively you will need to visit the Meridian Energy website, www.meridianenergy.co.nz. Here you will find links to information about how Meridian is developing wind energy in New Zealand. This should help you with the content of the essay.

Here is a collection of points that have been compiled to help you with your initial thinking and planning. You can use them to help you process the information from Meridian. Of course you may like to widen your search while you are on the Internet.

Feel free to argue whichever side of the issue you like.

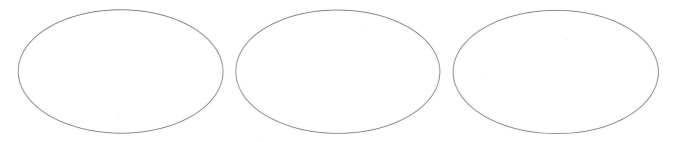

- Wind energy is now a well-proven technology.
- Noise has been reduced significantly through design breakthroughs.
- Unlikely to ever replace other forms of energy.
- 82% of those surveyed believed wind generation was the way of the future.
- Striking, impressive features on the landscape.
- Visually ugly.
- Reliability.
- Noise created by the rotor blades.
- Environmentally responsible.
- Fast to build.
- Bird mortality.

You do:

The body of the essay will have no fewer than three ideas in three separate paragraphs. Fill in this grid with the three paragraph topics you have chosen for your essay.

Paragraph Topic 1	
Paragraph Topic 2	
Paragraph Topic 3	

ISBN 9780170195928

Focus 2: Formal writing – writing a great paragraph

All great paragraphs will have:

- a topic sentence that states the idea
- an explanation saying in more detail what you meant in your topic sentence
- evidence that supports your explanation with an effective example. Anecdote, statistic, quotation, …
- a concluding connection to the topic.

You do:

Choose ONE paragraph from the essay you have planned. Write it in full using the grid below.

Topic sentence	What are you writing about?
Explanation	What do you mean?
Evidence	What makes you say that?
Connection to topic	So why is all that important?

ISBN 9780170195928

Week _____ Date for completion _____

Parent's sig. _____ Teacher's sig. _____

Focus 1: Creative writing

The aim of practising writing skills is to express yourself in a simple, accurate and interesting manner

Below is a writing starter on which to base a piece of narrative writing.

Read it carefully. Think:

- Who is the narrator? Boy? Girl? Age?
- What has he/she done?
- What is the 'prized object'?
- What happens in the next five minutes? It's your choice. You write the next part of this story.

Before you begin, take the time to brainstorm your ideas. Jot down spontaneous ideas, key words and phrases.

> I lay on my bed, staring at the ceiling, my entire body quaking with fear and adrenaline. What had I done? Why had I done it? I only know that I got a great sense of excitement from it. My breathing slowed to its normal rate, and I looked at the prized object clasped in my desperate childish fingers. ...

_____
_____
_____
_____
_____
_____
_____
_____
_____
_____
_____
_____
_____
_____
_____
_____
_____

Continue in the back of this book if you need more space.

ISBN 9780170195928

You can improve your spelling with regular practice. Spend some time this week learning these words. Learn the correct version of course!

Duz spelnk matr?

Short answer: Yes.

Long answer: You will not get far in school or in the competitive employment world if you cannot write coherent English with reasonably correct spelling. There will always be really hard words – that's where dictionaries help – but you must make every effort to spell well.

There are patterns in English, despite all the irregularities. We cannot do a lot of work here, but look at these examples:

1   When a word ends in 'y', it usually changes to 'i' before adding any ending:

story – stories
pity – pitiful
rely – reliable

Add an ending to these words:

lady   – _____

army   – _____

glory   – _____

supply   – _____

pretty   – _____

fury   – _____

You do:

Here is a list of words that are often spelt incorrectly. Write them correctly in the space provided. Then use a dictionary to see if you are right.

rythm   _____

parliment   _____

libary   _____

principul   _____

beatiful   _____

anoyed   _____

morgage   _____

neccessary   _____

behavior   _____

disapoint   _____

dissapear   _____

brekfast   _____

feild   _____

belive   _____

occassion   _____

vegitable   _____

wisper   _____

colum   _____

asignment   _____

fulfill   _____

Keep a list of your spelling corrections. Make sure you never misspell the same word twice!

2   In the accompanying textbook we talked about the differences between American and British spellings. Look at the list below and decide which is the commonly used spelling in New Zealand.

New Zealand English tends to follow British English spelling rules. Write the New Zealand English version of these words in the spaces provided:

American spelling	Usual New Zealand spelling
color	
labor	
aluminum	
plow	
favorite	
analyze	
center	
theater	

American spelling	Usual New Zealand spelling
skillful	
enrollment	
dialog	
aging	
judgment	
defense	
jewelry	
pajamas	

ISBN 9780170195928

Focus 1: Written close reading

By now you will have done some work honing your close reading skills. We assume you have worked through the exercises in the *How to ...* textbook and Unit 5 of this book. Go back to either for a recap on how to approach close reading of a written text.

Read the passage below and answer the questions that follow.

> The driver ants are carnivorous and nomadic. From time to time the army stops its march and when this happens, it disappears into various hiding places while scouts are sent out to explore the countryside. The information the scouts bring back helps them map their route. Once the route is decided, the order is given and <u>the earth belches ants</u>. A million pour out and form into line, roughly five abreast, and the advance begins. This is a very disciplined march. Along the ranks the big-headed soldiers, the officers, run directing the march, frequently meeting in little groups for apparent discussions.   5
>
> Nothing living will stop that column. Anything in its path is destroyed; even the gigantic python that can swallow a deer is killed and eaten if it does not get out of the way.   10
>
> A house is invaded silently, generally at night. Everything in that house that lives is killed. Before morning the ants will leave and the owner can return to find a house that is clean and all vermin, from rats to bugs, is wiped out – as also will be his poultry and stock if it is not set free – but food, other than meat, will be untouched.
>
> A man caught asleep is covered by the driver ants who do him no harm at all until presumably a signal is given. Then, all attack simultaneously. Each ant plunges in its pincers and pulls until the portion of flesh it has grasped comes out. That pincer grip never relaxes, even in death.   15
>
> The natives of the area, who might be miles away from medical help, put this tenacity of the ants to good use. When they have wounds that need to be stitched, they use the pincers of the driver ants to bind the edges together. It is a tricky job, but the ant is made to bite so that one pincer is on the one side of the cut and the other pincer on the other side. The closing pincers hold the edges of the wounds together and the ant's body is then cut off. It is most effective surgery.   20

1 The earth belches ants (line 4–5) means:

   a The ants go up in smoke.   c The earth is burping

   b The ants pour out of the ground.   d The ants are burping.   a   b   c   d

2 The ants like to eat meat. Find ONE word in the passage that means they eat meat. _____

3 Identify TWO things mentioned in the passage that the driver ants would eat.

   i _____   ii _____

4 The ants live in one area only. Is this statement true or false?

   _____

5 Find a quotation from the passage that supports your answer for Question 4.

_____

ISBN 9780170195928

6 Explain in your own words the role the scouts play.

_____

_____

7 Do the ants bite a person immediately if they find him asleep? Give evidence from the text to support your answer.

_____

_____

8 What does the word 'vermin', as used in line 13, mean? _____

9 Replace 'simultaneously' (line 16) with a word/phrase that has the same meaning.

_____

Focus 2: Homonyms and homophones

Homophones

Homophones are words that are pronounced in the same way, but differ in spelling and meaning. They are confusing words and often result in spelling errors.

For example:

We talk **aloud**.
We are **allowed** to go.

He **threw** the ball **through** the hoop.

He was **too** tired to play **two** matches.

The **principals** have high **principles**.

We buy school **stationery**.
The vehicle is **stationary**.

You may be wondering why you are being reminded about homophones. One very good reason is that you are probably using the computer spell-checker to check the accuracy of your writing. The problem many students encounter with computer spell-checkers is that they cannot choose the correct word for meaning, only for spelling. It is up to you to choose wisely.

Look at the following passage – a computer spell-checker would not recognise any errors. Hopefully you do. Rewrite it below correctly.

> Wee saw a sale at see. It seamed
> to bee hour principle's lit till craft
> but in thyme wee sore it was won
> bee longing to an udder person.

_____

_____

_____

_____

_____

Homonyms

Homonyms are words spelt and pronounced in an identical way, but they have different meanings and functions. Cryptic crosswords use them a lot.

The **bat** flew into the cave.
His cricket **bat** was brand new.
He will **bat** first for his team.

The first two sentences have the noun *bat*, but meaning different things, and the third is the verb *to bat*.

Fill in the gap in each section with the same word.

1 The dog has a loud _____.
   The _____ of the tree showed its age.

2 Judges should always try to be _____.
   There was plenty to buy at the _____.

3 The _____ are causing pollution.
   She _____ when she's angry.

4 The cargo was in the _____ of the ship.
   _____ my hand while we cross the road.

5 He is stuck in a traffic _____.
   Strawberry _____ is delicious on toast.
   Be careful not to _____ the paper in the printer.

In Unit 9 we asked you to learn the spelling of some commonly misspelt words. Get a parent, sibling or friend to test you on your ability to still remember these words.

Week _____ Date for completion _____
Parent's sig. _____ Teacher's sig. _____

Focus 1: Creating character notes

You will be asked to write about the main characters in text you study. It will be a lot easier to do this if you have first prepared some notes. Try the method below using the text you are currently studying in class.

What he/she looks like (5 min)

-
-
-
-
-
-

Something interesting the character says (5min)

Character drawing

What his/her problems are (5 min)

-
-
-
-
-
-

Describe his/her personality (5 min)

-
-
-
-
-
-

Use the information you have listed here to write a paragraph about the character. We have left you some space for planning. Write the final copy of your essay in the back of this book.

_____

_____

_____

_____

_____

ISBN 9780170195928

Focus 2: Paragraphing

A paragraph is formed from a group of sentences that have something in common; when put together they are linked as one part of an argument or the unfolding of a story.

You will often be reminded to use paragraphs effectively in your essay writing, keeping a single idea to a paragraph. Using paragraphs well helps to structure your essay in a logical order.

When you are writing creatively you need to recognise there are other places you need to use paragraphs too.

New paragraph for a change of speaker

When writing dialogue, it is essential to begin a new paragraph every time one person begins to speak. This lets the reader know who is speaking.

New paragraph for the passing of time

When an important passage of time has occurred, you begin a new paragraph.

New paragraph for a change of place

Characters in a story often move from one place to another. Whether or not a new paragraph is required depends upon how much the move affects the development of the story.

New paragraph for a new person

A new paragraph is usually required to introduce a person into a story. In some stories, a character is 'on stage' all the time; in others he or she may not be referred to for a few paragraphs. When the character returns to the story, a new paragraph is required only if he or she is important to the development of the plot.

> When you read anything, whether it is a textbook for Geography, a novel for English, a magazine article or a column in a newspaper, stop and look at the way the paragraphs are organised to make it easy for you to follow the writing and its ideas.

You do:

Read the passage below carefully. There should be six paragraphs. Using the information above circle the first word of each paragraph.

Stanley was asleep on the sofa in the living room in the middle of a hot summer afternoon. His head rested comfortably on his Mum's best cushion and his feet draped inelegantly over the sofa arm, hanging just above his cricket shoes. The front door slammed open and then, with even more force, shut. 'Stanley!' came the shrill voice of his grandmother. 'Stanley, where are you? I need you, right now!!!' The air in the living room around Stanley vibrated as the door swung open and Gran swept in. She might be small but she knew how to make an entrance. Her pink sunhat, purple flowered dress and white 'comfy' sandals filled Stanley's vision as he forced his eyes open. 'Ouch, don't pinch me,' he said, 'I'm awake already. I'm awake, what is it?' Stanley sat up and shook his head to clear it of the pleasant dream he'd been having about scoring the winning runs. Gran by now was in the armchair removing her sandals but not her hat. She liked to think it gave her an added air of authority. 'We've got a problem, Stan,' she said.

ISBN 9780170195928

Week _____ Date for completion _____

Parent's sig. _____ Teacher's sig. _____

Focus 1: Poetry writing – Diamantes

A Diamante is a poem or stanza of seven lines that follows a strict structure.

Light
limpid, keen
dazzling, sparkling, beaming
clarity, crystal, ebony, mystery
shrouding, obscuring, enveloping
shadowy, soft
Dark.

Line length	Content or purpose	Words
1 One word	names subject	noun
2 Two words	describes the subject in line 1	adjectives
3 Three words	describes the subject in line 1	participles (-ing, -ed)
4 Four words	first two relate to line 1 subject; second two relate to line 7 subject	nouns
5 Three words	describe the subject in line 7	participles (-ing, -ed)
6 Two words	describe the subject in line 7	adjectives
7 One word	names a subject that is the antonym of the line 1 subject	noun

Here are some more examples.

Use different-coloured highlighters to show the two parts of each poem.

Winter
frosty, bright
skiing, snowball fighting, sledding
icicles, snowflakes, vacation, family
swimming, sun tanning, sweltering
hot, sunny
Summer

Teenager
powerful, noisy
dancing, dating, consuming
explosion, energetic, maturity, senility
working, earning, saving
quiet, peaceful
Old-ager

Dreams
subconscious, imaginary
sleeping, wishing, thinking
fantasy, actuality, vision, genuine
being, seeing, knowing,
authentic, factual
Reality

ISBN 9780170195928

You do:

Draft your own Diamante poem and copy your final version on to the lines provided.

You may have an idea of something that will work already but if not, why not use one of our suggestions:

- starting schoolboy and finishing schoolgirl
- starting Mum and ending Dad
- starting Mum and ending Grandma/Nana
- starting city and ending country.

_____

_____

_____

_____

_____

_____

Focus 2: Adjectives

Adjectives are used a great deal in advertising. You will be asked to identify and explain them and you may well be asked to select some for advertisements of your own. Highlight all the adjectives you can see in these advertisements. Under each one say what it is about the product that the adjectives focus on. The first is done for you as an example.

Packed with only the finest, freshest ingredients and triple concentrated for maximum flavour, Leggo's Tomato Paste will bring out the very best in your favourite dishes.

Focus: quality and taste

Nutra-Life Hi-Omega Flaxseed Oil is 100% pure High-Omega 3 Flaxseed Oil, cold-pressed from special organically grown whole flaxseed. Nutra-Life Hi-Omega Flaxseed Oil helps to maintain circulation and healthy vibrant skin.

Focus: _____

Germ-X is an instant waterless hand sanitiser that kills 99.99% of common harmful germs and bacteria that can make you sick. It works in as little as 15 seconds, leaving your hands feeling clean, pleasant smelling and moisturised with vitamin E. Germ-X, it pays you to keep it on hand.

Focus: _____

Have soft, smooth, glowing skin all year round when you apply JOHNSON'S Holiday Skin every day. This ground-breaking new formula moisturises your skin while building a light natural-looking tan. JOHNSON'S Holiday Skin hydrates the skin for all-day moisturisation, while a small amount of self tan builds a natural-looking golden colour, without the fuss and smell of self-tanning lotions. Now you can have glowing skin all year round.

Focus: _____

ISBN 9780170195928

Focus 1: Analyse a review

THE GOOD, THE BAD AND THE DUSTY

For this review, we tried to ask all our friends who'd been to the event to write their intelligent thoughts down to help us get a well rounded perspective of experiences at Rhythm and Vines. Unfortunately their thoughts were not very intelligent and by the time we censored all the scandalous references about chicks, booze and other naughties, we were left with comments about the dust. And yes, Rhythm and Vines was very dusty and it seems it has settled in many memories as a major player of the event. What I couldn't believe was the property owners wanted to turn their beautiful landscape into a potential mud hole … could they not have planted grass? Perhaps the decision to extend the party to 10,000 punters was such a last minute decision that they just enlisted the help of a bulldozer. I guess the dust did add a 'smokey' atmosphere. However by the end of the night I looked like a dirty, smelly tramp.

Dust aside, the venue was fairly well arranged. As an R&V old timer, I was kind of bummed that the intimacy of previous years was lost to a 'show ground' affair. The space was immense and included a water slide, food and bev stands and possibly the best toilets I've ever experienced at an outdoor event. Seriously, the toilets were awesome. They flushed.

…

Now to more serious things … the music and vibe. The energy of the event was immense. Everyone was excited and on big adventures. Highlights for me were Kors, Sola Rosa, Freq Nasty, Pitch Black and Fat Freddy's. The general vibe though seemed to be that people were craving a few more dancey dancey acts. Many commented that the music was too mellow.

Fortunately some were lucky enough to stumble across DJ Phully who was playing to almost no one during the Fat Freddy's gig. I caught his last two tracks and was like, 'this guy is awesome', and then he finished.

…

At about 3am, Gizzy got incredibly cold. It seemed that most people were not prepared for the night temperatures as it plummeted below comfort level for those who had lost their tops or who had worn hot pants and singlets to cope with the day time heat. All I remember is shivering chicks and guys who had found random bits of material or signage lying around, covering themselves and heading for their cars. Bummer, they missed the best bit.

There is nothing more beautiful than watching the sun disappear behind the cornfields and then reappear above the vines. By sunrise, the few people who were left, grabbed their little tents and headed for the small stage to take in the last act, watch the sunrise, chill out and reflect upon their night. I think most people absolutely loved it and if a big party's your thing for New Years, check it out next year as it will be even bigger.

ISBN 9780170195928

1 Look at the tone created in this review. What does it suggest about

   a the author? _____

   b the audience? _____

2 Review titles are often catchy. Explain what is catchy about this one. (Clue: Ask your parents!)

_____

_____

3 Choose two different-coloured highlighters and highlight the positive things and then the negative things that have been talked about in this review.

Focus 2: How to write ... a film review

Your task this week is to write a review for one of the following:

- A film you are going to see at the theatre (so as you can watch carefully and jot down some quick notes immediately after the session).
- A DVD you choose for over the weekend.
- A film that you will watch on one of the television channels.

Note: Do not choose a film you have seen already, even if it was only last week. It is important that the film you work with has been watched critically, not just for leisure.

When writing a film review, there are several different guidelines to follow. Carefully read the information below before you begin your review.

Go back to chapter 7 of the *How to ...* text and reread the appropriate pages on writing reviews.

A generic outline

This outline will help you get going. Assume you are writing for your classmates. Your audience will determine the style, structure and length of your review.

Title	Catchy, you can play with words to make it funny or different.
Para 1	Opening paragraph – can start to summarise film and give early suggestions about your general review of it.
Para 2	Start or continue summary of film; don't give details about the end or else no one will go and see the film!
Para 3-4	Positive things you thought about the film. What did you like? Why?
Para 5-6	Negative things you thought about the film. What did you not like? Why?
Para 7	Characterisation – talk about the characters. Did you like them? Did the actors play them well? Will certain audience members not like certain characters? Why not?
Para 8	Final comments – general comments that summarise your view of the film. You may want to say something inspiring to get the reader to want to go out and see the film.
Rating	At the end you could give your film a star rating to indicate your overall opinion of the product.

ISBN 9780170195928

Week _____ Date for completion _____

Parent's sig. _____ Teacher's sig. _____

Focus 1: Making a visual image

New Zealand Post is frequently updating the look of its stamps. We are going to give you a chance to design a stamp which reflects/illustrates a place or concept that is significant to you about your own country.

You may pick any conventional stamp shape or size, although we suggest you enlarge the stamp to make it easier for you to work with.

Try and make your stamp look as professional as possible. Do not forget to include: a white border, a money 'amount', and the words 'New Zealand'.

Keep the following things in mind.

What style is your stamp going to be?

Photographic
Collage
Modern
Sketched
Symbolic

Let's recap ...

- Plan the layout, size, shape, colours of the static image.
- Decide on symbols/main images.
- Carefully choose the words to appear on the static image.
- Use materials that work well for the message.
- Use tools (ruler, set square, good scissors, photocopier, and so on) if you need to.

How are you going to incorporate visual techniques?

Colour
Contrast
Font (style and size)
Layout
Point of impact
Illustration/graphic
Unusual images
Symbols

Go back to chapter 14 of your *How to ...* book to look at more ideas on style and illustrations.

What technology are you going to use?

Travel brochures
Magazines
Felts
Paint
Computer graphics

Once you have completed your postage stamp we suggest you glue it into the inside back cover of this book. Then answer the following questions.

1 What **colours** did you choose and why?

_____

_____

_____

2 What is the **dominant visual feature** of your image? What was the effect you were trying to achieve?

_____

_____

_____

_____

3 Describe the **layout** of your image and explain the reasons behind your choices. For instance, why have you chosen to put your pictures where you have?

_____

_____

_____

_____

_____

ISBN 9780170195928

Focus 2: Visual and verbal techniques

It is important for you to learn the basic verbal and visual techniques commonly used in the production of visual text. Below is an exercise to help you begin the process. Link the term with the correct definition in the grid below.

	Answer	Term
a		**Colour**
b		**Alliteration**
c		**Font (style and size)**
d		**Layout**
e		**DVF**
f		**Graphic/illustration**
g		**Symbols/logos**
h		**Background**

	Answer	Term
i		**Empty space**
j		**Well-known/popular faces**
k		**Body copy**
l		**Repetition**
m		**Use of adjectives**
n		**Personal pronouns**
o		**Slogan**
p		**Rhetorical question**

Definitions

1   Where a concrete object is used to represent one or more abstract ideas.

2   The dominant colour used as the base of the image. It may be left plain in order to focus the viewer's attention on the other features or it may incorporate colour to support its message.

3   The pictures, photographs, drawings, graphs – everything that is not just the writing in an image.

4   Can be used to help represent their product or idea. It can also be eye-catching.

5   The use of words such as 'you', 'we', 'our' to give a chatty, conversational tone to the piece to make the audience feel included.

6   Carefully chosen describing words that help us picture the look, taste or texture of the product.

7   The use of someone who is famous to sell a product/service. It may be purely to attract our attention or to endorse a product.

8   The repetition of the product name, slogan and/or key features to help ingrain the brand in your mind.

9   The detailed words in a visual text.

10   The central focus (point of impact) of the visual text.

11   Will reflect the ideas within the image. Must also be easy to read.

12   A short, snappy sentence that sums up a product or service. It is usually easy to remember.

13   Used to allow the audience to focus on and consider the posed question.

14   Used most commonly because it is easy to remember. It makes words flow together more easily and highlights key words and ideas.

15   The process of organising the forms, shapes, colours and any words into a balanced design. These choices are made with the purpose, topic and audience in mind.

16   Where nothing is printed. It is critical in helping highlight graphics and illustrations.

43

ISBN 9780170195928

Focus 1: Visual close reading

A comic strip is a series of cartoon drawings narrating an incident. They are usually humorous and appear first in magazines or newspapers. They have conventions, for example in the way speech and thoughts are shown, in the way loud sounds or movement are indicated. You can see all of these in the *Footrot Flats* example here.

1 What evidence is there that this is a cartoon set on a farm?

_____

_____

2 In which frame does Dog shout the loudest?

_____

3 How does Murray Ball show that the fox terrier is still a puppy?

_____

_____

4 Find an example of colloquial (informal) language.

_____

5 What does the cartoonist do to make sure that we know that Dog is thinking all this rather than talking like the boy, Rangi, does?

_____

_____

Focus 2: Recap parts of speech

Read the following extract and find ONE example of the language features listed below.

This piano rocks. It's better than the one at home and infinitely better than Todd's one – I don't know why they keep a piano in a garage anyway. I play and play and I can feel the stress slip out of my feet and my fingers, the music taking it and chucking it away.

I pull out the manuscript and start on the music we've worked through again and again. I close my eyes and can hear Todd count us in Two, Three, Four then Michael and Chris starting in with drums and acoustic, one, two, three, four, I'm counting, hearing them and waiting for the eighth bar for me and Todd, one, two, three, four, then it's my turn. Da Da break. Da … Da, Da Da! Then, I'm away, into the melody, the one we wrote together and I can hear him singing.

Playing and playing and playing right to the end. Michael's down beat once with Chris pushing through that last chord change and me waiting, hearing them, waiting till it's my turn to do the solo with just me and Todd … right to the end, light, sweeter, gentle, gentle, slower and then just me finishing, bringing it to closure.

Perfect.

From G-Force, Tania Roxborogh

Parts of speech

Nouns

– Concrete _____

– Proper _____

– Abstract _____

Personal pronoun _____

Adjective _____

Verb _____

Apostrophe for contraction _____

Apostrophe for possession _____

Figurative language

Alliteration _____

Personification _____

Repetition _____

Sentences

A sentence written to suggest speed _____

_____

A sentence written to suggest slowness _____

_____

Look at chapter 2 of *How to …* to remind yourself of this.

45

Week _____ Date for completion _____
Parent's sig. _____ Teacher's sig. _____

HINT FOR SUCCESS
Don't think that once you've put your pen down you're finished. Not until you have spent time editing and streamlining your essay are you finished – even in an examination!

Focus 1: Character essay

This activity asks you to write a clear, detailed, thoughtful essay. Complete the information in the box below before you begin.

Title of text: [   ]   Author of text: [   ]

Let's recap how to write a literary essay

By now you will be aware of the basic structure you can use to write your essay.

Don't forget to use quotations to support your ideas. Go to page 98 of your *How to ...* textbook to remind yourself on how to best incorporate quotations in your essay.

Introduction
This paragraph should always:
- give the title and author (director, poet) of the text
- give the genre (novel, short story, poem, film)
- refer to the question.

Body paragraphs
The body of the essay is divided into paragraphs. How many will depend on the type of question you're asked. Generally a body paragraph should have:
- a topic sentence that clearly states what the paragraph will be about
- detail from the text
- relevant quotations
- explanation
- a sentence to link back to the original idea.

Conclusion
This will include:
- no new information (it shows a lack of prior planning)
- a restatement of the main point of your essay, strongly referring back to the question.

Let's have a look at the essay topic you have been given.

> Describe an idea that interested you in the text. Explain why it interested you.

Using a red or blue pen, annotate the question with the following:
- Put brackets around each part of the question.
- Underline the key words in the question.

In the box below decide upon the following things:
- List two possible relationships you could use for this topic. Think about main character(s) and their relationship with each other and with minor characters.
- For each relationship, brainstorm at least two reasons why this relationship was important to the text.
- Think about some of the following things: Did the relationship change? Did the relationship offer support to one character or both characters? Did it illustrate the idea/purpose/theme? Did the relationship create conflict/humour? Did the relationship reveal a character's personality or values?

ISBN 9780170195928

| Relationship 1 _____ and_____ | |
| Relationship 2 _____ and_____ | |

Evaluate the information you have in the box above. One relationship should stand out as being easier to write about than the others.

- Look through your handouts, character notes, and so on.
- Go back to the key places in the text and reread them. Take notes and copy suitable quotations.
- Use a different-colour pen to group and structure your information.

You should now be ready to begin writing your essay. Write the final copy of your essay in the back of this book.

Focus 2: Verbs

Verbs

You will all know that a verb is a 'doing' or a 'being' word. Verbs are really very important because they can tell us so much. Imagine you are watching someone walk down the street. This person's **way of walking** can say so much. Is he:

ambling?	Suggests carefree, not in a hurry, no particular purpose.
hurrying?	Suggests late for something, worried, panicked.
skipping?	Suggests happy, lively, young, enjoyment.
limping?	Suggests injury, pain, discomfort, age.
shambling?	Suggests a tramp, a lack of motor control, a lack of purpose.

When you're searching for a good word, a thesaurus is a marvellous help.

A verb is so valuable and it's worth taking the time to choose just the right one.

You do:

What do these verbs suggest to you?

crawled _____

dashed _____

hiked _____

stormed _____

trudged _____

Now try finding some alternatives to the well-used word *said*. Include what you want the word to suggest.

1 _____   _____

2 _____   _____

3 _____   _____

4 _____   _____

5 _____   _____

47

ISBN 9780170195928

Week _____ Date for completion _____

Parent's sig. _____ Teacher's sig. _____

Focus 1: Speech planning

Use the following activity to help formulate the ideas and structure of your speech.

Your topic is: _____

Remember to structure your speech

Opening

- Gets the audience's attention.
- Tells the audience what the topic is.
- Tells the audience what points to listen for. They are

_____

_____

_____

Your first point is

_____

_____

_____

- Backed up with what type of evidence?

_____

Your second point is

_____

_____

_____

- Backed up with what type of evidence?

_____

Your third point is

_____

_____

_____

- Backed up with what type of evidence?

_____

Conclusion

- Summarises the presentation.
- Emphasises what you want the audience to remember, which is:

_____

_____

_____

You need to open your speech effectively. It is important that your audience wants to continue listening to your speech. Try to think of one each of the following for your topic.

- Shock them with a statistic/fact _____
- Ask a question _____
- Use a quotation _____

You must back up your points with evidence. Try and incorporate a different method for each point you make. Try and think of one of each of the following for your topic.

- Statistics _____
- Historical facts _____
- A story (anecdote) _____
- Current event _____

You might like to incorporate some of the following into the body of your speech to make it more interesting. Write some sentences about your topic that use the features below.

- Alliteration _____
- Similes _____
- Onomatopoeia _____

You need to ensure your audience remembers your speech. Try and include something that will hold in their mind after you have finished speaking. Try to think of one each of the following for your topic.

- Remind them of a shocking statistic _____
- Ask a rhetorical question _____
- Use a quote _____

Show this information to your teacher before you go any further with your speech.

48

ISBN 9780170195928

1. Rhetorical question

Speakers often use a rhetorical question at the beginning or end of their speech. At the beginning of the speech you can ask a question that will capture your audience's attention and get them involved in your speech and thinking about how it is relevant to them.

For example: *How many of you suffer from 'Bad Hair Days'?* (pause) *I can see many of you nodding your head ...*

By using a rhetorical question at the end of your speech you will leave your audience something to think about. It may provoke them to make a change in their lives or to consider the issue beyond the end of your speech.

For example: *So, what will you do with your empty bottle next time you are faced with the dilemma of there being no bin in sight?*

2. Listing

Listing provides your audience with lots of examples, adding weight to your argument.

For example: *Whether it is you or I, Bono or Bob Geldof, Kofi Annan or Tony Blair, Angelina Jolie or the various statesmen for the African nations at the centre of this issue, it is firmly believed by a majority of people that something must be done about the crisis facing Africa today.*

In the above example the speech writer wanted to show that people from all walks of life, status and importance agree with the issue – emphasising that is not something trivial.

You do:

Use the following information to help you write a short (100-word) section of a speech on the topic 'The Importance of Recycling' that contains a rhetorical question and an example of listing.

Recycling is a process of making waste into new and different products.

Glass can become many things once recycled, so can paper.

Many people recycle plastic bottles and aluminium cans.

When shopping, remember to buy products that are recyclable or have recyclable packaging.

Avoid landfills.

Industry is good at recycling steel.

Kerbside collections.

The North Shore City Council collects about 16,339 tonnes of recyclables per year.

Reduce it. Reuse it. Recycle!

It will help to reduce future disposal costs.

Inorganic collections.

_____

_____

_____

_____

_____

_____

_____

_____

_____

_____

ISBN 9780170195928

Focus 1: Visual close reading

Whatever spins your wheels

use of celebrity
• Sarah Ulmer
• Evers-Swindel twins

...or floats your boat!

With so many quick and easy ways to prepare lean beef and lamb, you can choose exactly what you feel like and feel twice as good!

connects to:

BEEF + LAMB
Feel Twice as Good
www.recipes.co.nz

ISBN 9780170195928

Read the advertisement through carefully. There is a space to label each of these techniques on the advert. Fill in the gaps.

Layout
- Headline
- Image
- Body copy
- Background
- Logo/slogan

Verbal techniques
Pronouns
Alliteration
Rhyme
Adjectives
Repetition
Slogan
Pun/play on words

Visual techniques
Empty space
Headline
DVF
Use of celebrity
Symbol

Now you have spent some time analysing the advertisement, answer the questions that follow.

1 Explain the connection between the headline 'Whatever spins your wheels … or floats your boat' to the rest of the image.

_____
_____
_____
_____

2 Explain the connection of the phrase 'so many quick and easy ways to prepare lean beef and lamb' to the rest of the image.

_____
_____
_____
_____

Focus 2: Punctuation practice

Read the passage and then answer the questions that follow.

For nearly fifty years, Scott Base has been New Zealand's base in Antarctica. It houses about eighty people over the summer, although only about ten or twelve of them stay for the long dark winter. Many of them are scientists, but there are also support staff, who all have important jobs – people like chefs, kitchen hands, cleaners, mechanics and engineers.

Explain why each numbered punctuation mark has been used:

1 _____
2 _____
3 _____
4 _____
5 _____

ISBN 9780170195928

Week _____ Date for completion _____
Parent's sig. _____ Teacher's sig. _____

Focus 1: Sentences make sense

Read this passage:

It is one thousand years ago a moa walks out of a South Island forest and into scrubland it is very wary looking repeatedly at the sky it begins feeding on smaller plants pruning them like hedge clippers This moa is the biggest flightless bird in the world it weighs almost 200 kilograms nearly twice the weight of Jonah Lomu for the moment, it thinks it's safe it isn't

Not that easy, is it? If you read it aloud you will naturally put in pauses to make it make sense.

When people talk to you, they put in pauses to make what they are saying easy to understand. It's the same with writing: the punctuation is there to help the reader get to the meaning of the words easily as he or she reads.

You do:

Rewrite the passage above using full stops, commas and capital letters to make it easier to understand.

_____
_____
_____
_____
_____
_____
_____
_____

If you know you have trouble with sentences, here's another passage where the full stops and capital letters are missing. Read the passage aloud to see what it means and then put in the punctuation.

Try and be vigilant with your full stops this week.

horses are wonderful they're so beautiful but I can't have one, even though I really, really want one I don't even ask it costs a lot of money to buy a horse and then more to feed it and to pay to use a paddock we don't have that kind of money

what I do instead is I draw horses I love to draw them I have a special artist's block with stiff, thick, white paper in it my mum gave it to me for my birthday I draw my best pictures in there I take a lot of time and use only pencil, and I rub out really carefully so I don't make a mess

ISBN 9780170195928

Focus 2: Prepositions and conjunctions

Let's stop and take another look at the 'little' words that help hold a sentence together.

Prepositions

A preposition's job in a sentence is to join nouns or pronouns to other words in a sentence. Prepositions show relationships (for example the place, direction or distance) between one thing or person and another. One good way to remember this is prepositions show position.

Examples of prepositions are:

in	out	under	over	beside	between	towards	across
about	inside	without	through	beneath	into	up	down

You do:

Write the directions for getting from your house to the nearest beach (or supermarket, if you don't live next to the beach). Use at least five prepositions like 'down', 'across', 'under', 'beside' and 'over'.

_____

_____

_____

_____

_____

Conjunctions

Essentially a conjunction glues parts of a sentence together. Conjunctions are connecting words that join two or more sentences into a single sentence. They can also join words, phrases or clauses.

Joining two words:	The day was sunny **and** windy.
Joining two sentences to make one sentence:	It was perfect for sailing **so** we headed for the marina.

Conjunctions are usually found in the middle of sentences, but some may be used to begin a sentence.

> The boat sailed beautifully well **although** it was small.
> could be written as:
> **Although** the boat was small, it sailed beautifully well.

Choosing the correct conjunction depends on what you want to say. Look at these examples:

> Jean likes toast **and** cereal for breakfast.
> Jean likes toast **but** prefers cereal for breakfast.
> Jean likes toast **or** cereal for breakfast.

Each sentence says something different because of the conjunction that has been chosen.

You do:

Using these four conjunctions create four different sentences.

and   **as**   **after**   **before**

1 Every day _____ he goes to school, Sam does his paper round.

2 Every day Sam goes to school _____ does his paper round.

3 Every day Sam goes to school _____ he does his paper round.

4 _____ Sam goes to school, he does his paper round.

53

ISBN 9780170195928

Week _____ Date for completion _____

Parent's sig. _____ Teacher's sig. _____

Focus 1: Understanding poetry

Have go at translating this poem in the space provided on the right-hand side of the page.

Fone Filosfy

Phone Philosophy _____

luv

is a nrvus rng

Ch@rin thru yr ♥

wearing valvt sliprs

n a roz bhin hr ear

hidin a chocl8 bx bhin hr bak

shock

a sombr call

stmpin n da door

@ 2 in da morn

wakin da dog n naybrs

leavn a blak egd telgrm

n da dorstp

xitmnt

s a rng

dat swoops n swrls

n rozy culrs roun ur cheeks

btrflyn tru ur tum

n life

is axeptin dat sumtims

silnce

cn say mor dn ny telfon

dat rngs 4 u

by Louise Phyn

The message of the poem is found in the last stanza. In your own words explain what you think the poet is saying.

_____

_____

_____

_____

_____

_____

ISBN 9780170195928

Focus 2: New languages – texting and emailing

Recent developments in technology such as email and cellphones have created a new language. The language of text and email is informal and generally does not adhere to grammatical rules.

You will find you use acronyms:

FAQ	Frequently Asked Questions	lol	laugh out loud
rofl	roll on floor laughing	DW	don't worry
TB	text back	ty	thank you
brb	be right back	btw	by the way
cu	see you		

You might even use emoticons:

:-)	happy/smiling	:-))	very happy
:-(	sad	:-o	surprised/shocked
:-O	bored	%-)	confused
:')	crying	;-P	Tongue in cheek

Be careful – it may be appropriate for you to use this style of language when texting or emailing but it is not appropriate for formal writing in essays, letters, and so on.

You do:

Have a go at either:

Writing a series of text messages that use e-language.

Or   Translating a piece of writing into e-language. (Don't forget to attach a copy of the original piece of writing.)

Or   Writing your own poem using e-language.

55

ISBN 9780170195928

Week _____ Date for completion _____

Parent's sig. _____ Teacher's sig. _____

Focus 1: Speech marks

Inverted commas

You know what these are but you may be more familiar with the name 'speech marks' or 'quotation marks'. These names come from what we use them for: to show in writing what is a quotation or what is direct speech.

The name inverted commas is because they are made of commas; the first one or set is up (") and the second is inverted, turned upside down (").

> You may use either one inverted comma or two. Just be sure that they match. If you use two at the beginning of a quotation you must use two at the end. So "…" or '…' – it's up to you.

> If you want to put a quotation within a quotation use single marks inside double marks. For example, "When I say 'now' I mean right this minute!" said Dad.

Using inverted commas in dialogue

Put the words actually spoken inside the speech marks. All other words are outside. For example:

> 'You boys all set for tomorrow?' asked Ms Lyons, our music teacher.

> Abe gave one of his huge grins. 'Man, we are the best!' he said. Tere and Reuben laughed and agreed. I smiled, too, but only on the outside.

Remember that all the punctuation belonging to the spoken words goes inside the speech marks. That's a little detail that trips students up – you read it here! Also remember that:

• the first word inside the inverted commas begins with a capital letter if it's the start of the speaker's words. If the spoken sentence is broken, then the second part will not use a capital letter. Here's an example:

> 'We're going to play brilliantly,' smiled Tere, 'and win!'

• you use a new paragraph for each new speaker.

You do:

Correctly punctuate the following passage. You will need to use capital letters, full stops, commas, apostrophes, inverted commas and an exclamation mark!

no way mum im not going vicky glared at the rusty van juddering down the farm road towards them there are heaps of kids in the back please dont make me get in with them

why not asked mum you might enjoy it id say theyre off to kill the pig for the birthday

ugh thats disgusting you want your only daughter to witness the killing of an innocent animal

the driver of the van must have noticed mums silver four-wheel-drive he waved and tooted and swung the wheel towards the gate

mum …vicky pleaded

it'll give you a chance to get to know some of the kids from the marae

ISBN 9780170195928

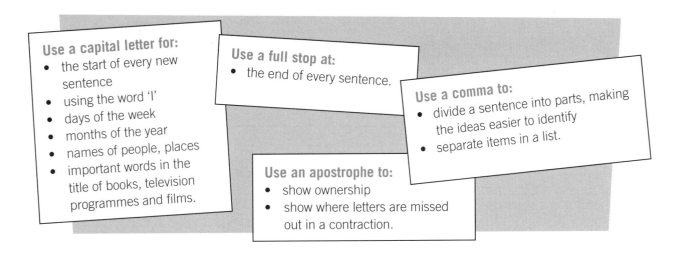

Use a capital letter for:
- the start of every new sentence
- using the word 'I'
- days of the week
- months of the year
- names of people, places
- important words in the title of books, television programmes and films.

Use a full stop at:
- the end of every sentence.

Use a comma to:
- divide a sentence into parts, making the ideas easier to identify
- separate items in a list.

Use an apostrophe to:
- show ownership
- show where letters are missed out in a contraction.

You do:

1 Correct the following paragraph, putting in the correct punctuation. It might be a good idea to start in pencil.

campbell island is the southernmost island of new zealand it lies on the 52nd parallel southeast of the auckland islands 600 kilometres from stewart island it is the remains of an extinct volcano its highest peak rises 550 metres above the southern ocean its western sides are steep with rocky ledges and sheer cliffs there are few sheltered coves and sandy bays the island slopes towards the east which is more sheltered from the strong westerly and antarctic winds in the frequent gales wind speed is around 34 knots (about 55 km per hour) gusting up to 70–80 knots (110–130 km per hour) with rain hail and sleet in a hurricane, gusts can rise to 240 km per hour it is often cold but even in the winter the snow doesnt stay around for long because the sea temperature of 7 or 8 degrees Celsius keeps the land warm the average annual temperature is 6 degrees and in the brief summer doesn't go much above 12 but the sky is light then until eleven at night

Just to be nice we thought we'd let you know that the author of this extract included:

20 capital letters   12 full stops   10 commas   1 apostrophe

ISBN 9780170195928

Week _____ Date for completion _____

Parent's sig. _____ Teacher's sig. _____

Focus 1: Who makes movies?

Use either the library or the Internet to help you complete the following exercise.

1   Describe what each of the following phases of film making are. Give some examples of tasks likely to be completed in each.

Pre-production _____

_____

Production _____

_____

Post-production _____

_____

2   What role does each of the following play in the pre-production, production or post-production of a film?

Producer _____

_____

Director _____

_____

Production assistant _____

_____

Director of photography/cinematography _____

_____

Grip _____

_____

Scriptwriter _____

_____

Editor _____

_____

Continuity _____

_____

Costume designer _____

_____

Foley editor _____

_____

Composer _____

_____

Gaffer _____

_____

Location manager _____

_____

ISBN 9780170195928

You all know that a pronoun takes the place of a noun. Let's take some time to recap pronouns.

Find the pronouns

Highlight all the pronouns. If you can, use two colours to show personal and possessive pronouns.

1   He went outside to find them.

2   We asked her if she was feeling all right.

3   Do you know if they want to come with us?

4   It isn't yours; it's mine!

5   They took me home in their car.

6   I will have dinner when they come home.

7   We didn't know if she was in our team.

8   He plays cricket for them every week.

Why a pronoun?

Ask yourself: *why* is a pronoun used? In the most straightforward situation a pronoun is to ensure that we are not irritated with having the same name repeated over and over again in a text, a conversation, a film: anywhere, in fact.

Here's the start of a children's story:

> Riley and Mia wanted to go into the garden and jump on the trampoline. Riley and Mia asked Mum if Riley and Mia could go outside. The only problem was Riley and Mia's mum had banned Riley and Mia from the tramp after Riley and Mia had spent all morning fighting over the smallest things. Riley had an idea. Riley whispered Riley's plan into Mia's ear. Mia nodded, and Riley and Mia crept under Riley and Mia's beds and tried to keep silent, waiting for Mum to start looking for Riley and Mia.

Put the pronouns 'he', 'she', 'they', 'their', 'he', 'she', 'them' in the spaces left for them and you will make the passage sound less repetitive.

> Riley and Mia wanted to go into the garden and jump on the trampoline. _____ asked Mum if _____ could go outside. The only problem was _____ mum had banned _____ from the tramp after _____ had spent all morning fighting over the smallest things. Riley had an idea. _____ whispered _____ plan into Mia's ear. _____ nodded, and _____ crept under _____ beds and tried to keep silent, waiting for Mum to start looking for _____.

Being able to use pronouns effectively will help you to improve your own writing.

ISBN 9780170195928

UNIT 23

Week _____ Date for completion _____

Parent's sig. _____ Teacher's sig. _____

HINT FOR SUCCESS
Those who read can (usually) spell: it's true!

Focus 1: Visual close reading – look and see

E kuri: Hey dog   Hikina te wero: Take up the challenge   Kokopu: native fish

This time we want you to identify the techniques for yourself. Read the advertisement through carefully and highlight/annotate the **layout** elements of a visual text.

Then look for as many examples of **verbal techniques** and **visual techniques** as you can possibly find. Make sure you do this tidily. Do not ruin your ability to see the overall image.

Visual techniques
Point of contrast
Bold lettering
Logos
Balance
Reverse type
Conventions of cartoons

Layout
- Headline
- Image
- Body copy
- Background
- Logo/slogan

Verbal techniques
Proper noun
Colloquial language
Cliché
Tone of language
Repetition
Use of adjectives for effect
Personal pronouns
Alliteration
Contraction
Maori (local flavour)

Focus 2: Visual close reading – questions

Now you have spent some time analysing the advertisement, answer the questions that follow.

1 There are two things being advertised in this advertisement. What are they?

_____

_____

_____

2 What is the connection between the two parts of the advertisement?

_____

_____

_____

3 How have they made the two sections of the advertisement different from each other?

_____

_____

_____

_____

4 How are the two parts of the advertisement joined together?

_____

_____

_____

_____

5 How many logos appear on the advertisement?

_____

61

ISBN 9780170195928

Focus: Putting it all together

All Summer in a Day

Ray Bradbury

'Ready?'

'Ready.'

'Now?'

'Soon.'

'Do the scientists really know? Will it happen today, will it?'

'Look, look; see for yourself!'

The children pressed to each other like so many roses, so many weeds, intermixed, peering out for a look at the hidden sun.

It rained.

It had been raining for seven years; thousands upon thousands of days compounded and filled from one end to the other with rain, with the drum and gush of water, with the sweet crystal fall of showers and the concussion of storms so heavy they were tidal waves come over the islands. A thousand forests had been crushed under the rain and grown up a thousand times to be crushed again. And this was the way life was forever on the planet Venus, and this was the schoolroom of the children of the rocket men and women who had come to a raining world to set up civilization and live out their lives.

'It's stopping, it's stopping!'

'Yes, yes!'

Margot stood apart from them, from these children who could never remember a time when there wasn't rain and rain and rain. They were all nine years old, and if there had been a day, seven years ago, when the sun came out for an hour and showed its face to the stunned world, they could not recall. Sometimes, at night, she heard them stir, in remembrance, and she knew they were dreaming and remembering gold or a yellow crayon or a coin large enough to buy the world with. She knew they thought they remembered a warmness, like a blushing in the face, in the body, in the arms and legs and trembling hands. But then they always awoke to the tatting drum, the endless shaking down of clear bead necklaces upon the roof, the walk, the gardens, the forests, and their dreams were gone.

All day yesterday they had read in class about the sun. About how like a lemon it was, and how hot. And they had written small stories or essays or poems about it:

I think the sun is a flower,
That blooms for just one hour.

That was Margot's poem, read in a quiet voice in the still classroom while the rain was falling outside.

'Aw, you didn't write that!' protested one of the boys.

'I did,' said Margot. 'I did.'

'William!' said the teacher.

But that was yesterday. Now the rain was slackening, and the children were crushed in the great thick windows.

Where's teacher?'

'She'll be back.'

'She'd better hurry, we'll miss it!'

They turned on themselves, like a feverish wheel, all tumbling spokes. Margot stood alone. She was a very frail girl who looked as if she had been lost in the rain for years and the rain had washed out the blue from her eyes and the red from her mouth and the yellow from her hair. She was an old photograph dusted from an album, whitened away, and if she spoke at all her voice would be a ghost. Now she stood, separate, staring at the rain and the loud wet world beyond the huge glass.

'What're *you* looking at?' said William.

Margot said nothing.

'Speak when you're spoken to.'

He gave her a shove. But she did not move; rather she let herself be moved only by him and nothing else. They edged away from her, they would not look at her. She felt them go away. And this was because she would play no games with them in the echoing tunnels of the underground city. If they tagged her and ran, she stood blinking after them and did not follow. When the class sang songs about happiness and life and games her lips barely moved. Only when they sang about the sun and the summer did her lips move as she watched the drenched windows. And then, of course, the biggest crime of all was that she had come here only five years ago from Earth, and she remembered the sun and the way the sun was and the sky was when she was four in Ohio. And they, they had been on Venus all their lives, and they had been only two years old when last the sun came out and had long since forgotten the colour and heat of it and the way it really was.

But Margot remembered.

'It's like a penny,' she said once, eyes closed.

'No it's not!' the children cried.

'It's like a fire,' she said, 'in the stove.'

'You're lying, you don't remember!' cried the children.

But she remembered and stood quietly apart from all of them and watched the patterning windows. And once, a month ago, she had refused to shower in the school shower rooms, had clutched her hands to her ears and over her head, screaming the water mustn't touch her head. So after that, dimly, dimly, she sensed it, she was different and they knew her difference and kept away. There was talk that her father and mother were taking

ISBN 9780170195928

her back to Earth next year; it seemed vital to her that they do so, though it would mean the loss of thousands of dollars to her family. And so, the children hated her for all these reasons of big and little consequence. They hated her pale snow face, her waiting silence, her thinness, and her possible future.

'Get away!' The boy gave her another push. 'What're you waiting for?'

Then, for the first time, she turned and looked at him. And what she was waiting for was in her eyes.

'Well, don't wait around here!' cried the boy savagely. 'You won't see nothing!'

Her lips moved.

'Nothing!' he cried. 'It was all a joke, wasn't it?' He turned to the other children. 'Nothing's happening today. *Is* it?'

They all blinked at him and then, understanding, laughed and shook their heads.

'Nothing, nothing!'

'Oh, but,' Margot whispered, her eyes helpless. 'But this is the day, the scientists predict, they say, they *know*, the sun …'

'All a joke!' said the boy, and seized her roughly. 'Hey, everyone, let's put her in a closet before the teacher comes!'

'No,' said Margot, falling back.

They surged about her, caught her up and bore her, protesting, and then pleading, and then crying, back into a tunnel, a room, a closet, where they slammed and locked the door. They stood looking at the door and saw it tremble from her beating and throwing herself against it. They heard her muffled cries. Then, smiling, they turned and went out and back down the tunnel, just as the teacher arrived.

'Ready, children?' She glanced at her watch.

'Yes!' said everyone.

'Are we all here?'

'Yes!'

The rain slacked still more.

They crowded to the huge door.

The rain stopped.

It was as if, in the midst of a film concerning an avalanche, a tornado, a hurricane, a volcanic eruption, something had, first, gone wrong with the sound apparatus, thus muffling and finally cutting off all noise, all of the blasts and repercussions and thunders, and then, second, ripped the film from the projector and inserted in its place a beautiful tropical slide which did not move or tremor. The world ground to a standstill. The silence was so immense and unbelievable that you felt your ears had been stuffed or you had lost your hearing altogether. The children put their hands to their ears. They stood apart. The door slid back and the smell of the silent, waiting world came in to them.

The sun came out.

It was the colour of flaming bronze and it was very large. And the sky around it was a blazing blue tile colour. And the jungle burned with sunlight as the children, released from their spell, rushed out, yelling, into the springtime.

'Now, don't go too far,' called the teacher after them.

'You've only two hours, you know. You wouldn't want to get caught out!'

But they were running and turning their faces up to the sky and feeling the sun on their cheeks like a warm iron; they were taking off their jackets and letting the sun burn their arms.

'Oh, it's better than the sun lamps, isn't it?'

'Much, much better!'

They stopped running and stood in the great jungle that covered Venus, that grew and never stopped growing, tumultuously, even as you watched it. It was a nest of octopi, clustering up great arms of fleshlike weed, wavering, flowering in this brief spring. It was the colour of rubber and ash, this jungle, from the many years without sun. It was the colour of stones and white cheeses and ink, and it was the colour of the moon.

The children lay out, laughing, on the jungle mattress, and heard it sigh and squeak under them resilient and alive. They ran among the trees, they slipped and fell, they pushed each other, they played hide-and-seek and tag, but most of all they squinted at the sun until the tears ran down their faces; they put their hands up to that yellowness and that amazing blueness and they breathed of the fresh, fresh air and listened and listened to the silence which suspended them in a blessed sea of no sound and no motion. They looked at everything and savoured everything. Then, wildly, like animals escaped from their caves, they ran and ran in shouting circles. They ran for an hour and did not stop running.

And then –

In the midst of their running one of the girls wailed.

Everyone stopped.

The girl, standing in the open, held out her hand.

'Oh, look, look,' she said, trembling.

They came slowly to look at her opened palm.

In the centre of it, cupped and huge, was a single raindrop. She began to cry, looking at it. They glanced quietly at the sun.

'Oh. Oh.'

A few cold drops fell on their noses and their cheeks and their mouths. The sun faded behind a stir of mist. A wind blew cold around them. They turned and started to walk back toward the underground house, their hands at their sides, their smiles vanishing away.

A boom of thunder startled them and like leaves before a new hurricane, they tumbled upon each other and ran. Lightning struck ten miles away, five miles away, a mile, a half mile. The sky darkened into midnight in a flash.

They stood in the doorway of the underground for a moment until it was raining hard. Then they closed the door and heard the gigantic sound of the rain falling in tons and avalanches, everywhere and forever.

'Will it be seven more years?'

'Yes. Seven.'

Then one of them gave a little cry.

'Margot!'

'What?'

'She's still in the closet where we locked her.'

'Margot.'

ISBN 9780170195928

They stood as if someone had driven them, like so many stakes, into the floor. They looked at each other and then looked away. They glanced out at the world that was raining now and raining and raining steadily. They could not meet each other's glances. Their faces were solemn and pale. They looked at their hands and feet, their faces down.

'Margot.'

One of the girls said, 'Well …?'

No one moved.

'Go on,' whispered the girl.

They walked slowly down the hall in the sound of cold rain. They turned through the doorway to the room in the sound of the storm and thunder, lightning on their faces, blue and terrible. They walked over to the closet door slowly and stood by it.

Behind the closet door was only silence.

They unlocked the door, even more slowly, and let Margot out.

Task 1: Understanding the story

1 What does this passage show about the change in the students' attitude?

'They stood as if someone had driven them with so many stakes into the floor. They looked at each other and then looked away … They could not meet each other's glances. Their faces were solemn and pale. They looked at their hands and feet, their faces down.'

  a They now feel sorry for Margot.

  b They are sad about the rain starting again so soon.

  c They now realise how cruel they have been.

  d All of the above.

  e None of the above.

a   b   c   d   e

2 What does the title of the story mean?

  a It all happened on a summer day.

  b Since the period of sun was so short, the kids were forced to live a whole summer in a day.

  c The summer seemed like it lasted only a day.

  d The days are long in the summer.

a   b   c   d

3 What point is made about Margot when the story says that the rain had washed 'the blue from her eyes and the red from her mouth and the yellow from her hair'?

  a The lack of sun is making her pale.

  b She hated the rain.

  c She was very sensitive to rain.

  d The rain was draining the life out of her.

a   b   c   d

4 Locking Margot up is especially mean because …

  a she is afraid of the dark.

  b sunshine is so rare on this planet.

  c she has no friends.

  d she cries when she is locked up.

a   b   c   d

5 The main purpose of the story is probably …

  a to provide a picture of what everyday life on Venus might be like.

  b to show how weather conditions can affect your personality.

  c to show how nine-year-old kids are.

  d to show how differences can make some people a target for others.

a   b   c   d

6 Margot's background makes her feel …

  a different from her classmates.

  b better than her classmates.

  c sympathetic toward her classmates because they haven't seen the sun.

  d angry toward her classmates.

a   b   c   d

ISBN 9780170195928

7 The *main* conflict of the story was …
   a the kids of Venus vs. the rain and nature.
   b William vs. Margot.
   c The kids vs. someone different.
   d Margot vs. the teacher for not helping her.
   e the kids vs. themselves.

a   b   c   d   e

8 The first thing the kids notice as soon as the rain stops is …
   a the warmth.
   b the brightness.
   c the mud everywhere.
   d the silence.

a   b   c   d

9 Ray Bradbury compares the jungle on Venus to …
   a tentacles of an octopus.
   b the colour of white cheese.
   c the colour of the moon.
   d all of the above.
   e none of the above.

a   b   c   d   e

10 When the kids open the door at the end, Margot's most likely reaction would be …
   a to scream and attack William for making her miss the sun.
   b to run outside into the rain.
   c to sit in the corner of the closet crying.
   d to yell at the teacher to punish William and the kids.

a   b   c   d

Choose ONE of the following tasks

A Character

Write a brief character study of Margot. Include the following:

- Her physical appearance
- Her personality
- Her relationship to others.

> Use the pages at the back of this book to write your final copy.

B Theme

Write a 200–250 word essay which explores what this short story tells you about either:

   How individuality can lead to jealousy.

   OR

   How discrimination hurts people.

Try to apply the ideas in the story to your classroom world here on Earth.

C Creative writing

One of the effective techniques in *All Summer in a Day* is Ray Bradbury's ability to describe the setting of Venus before and while the sun comes out. To do this he uses many of the language techniques listed above. Your job is to write a passage in a similar descriptive style as 'All Summer in a Day'. You do not need to involve characters, just concentrate on setting. You can choose between:

- A grey world where for only one day every seven years colours appear.
- A very windy world where the wind stops for three hours every seven years.

You should attempt to involve as many language techniques as you can (without going overboard). You should aim to write about three-quarters of a page. You should start with a rough copy but make sure that you correct your punctuation and spelling once finished.

ISBN 9780170195928

Week _____ Date for completion _____

Parent's sig. _____ Teacher's sig. _____

Focus: Putting it all together

Read the passage below and answer the questions that follow.

Winter and Summer in Bannockburn

Oliver Miller

On clear summer mornings in Bannockburn, the birds are so loud it sounds like a symphony orchestra. Frogs burp in the swamp at the base of the cliff in front of the lawn, and lizards, the length of pencils, bask on the pile of flat white stones by the hot tub. In the hazy distance, bald brown hills hunch like the bare bones of Gollum's back.

There is an old bathtub made of tin, which is always full of dirty rainwater and leaves, and it sits in the corner of the lawn. Tadpoles live in the bathtub, so sometimes, very early into the morning, a small neon-blue kingfisher comes and perches on the rim, dipping into the grubby water with his long, blade-shaped beak.

Beside the bathtub is a new, varnished, wooden hot tub, which is barely ever used in summer, so it sits there dormant like a volcano.

The wooden single-storied house has a large verandah, which is always full of odds and ends. An ancient out-of-tune piano, getting more so in the summer heat; a little tricycle covered in spider webs. There are beds with enormous mosquito nets hanging above them like ominous, grey rainclouds and boxes and boxes of tinned peaches lining the edge of the house.

When there has been a clear night, a heavy dew coats the grass, freezing desperate feet running for the out-house dunny. Later, on a hot day, a warm northerly wind starts to blow, and the tall poplars, on a ridge behind the house, shake and rustle their silvery leaves as if in jealousy of the sheltered, dusty pine down the drive.

Bannockburn is a place visited all year round. In winter the verandah is filled with boxes of driftwood and pinecones for the fire. Frost coats everything in the early morning and the birds are too cold to sing their songs. The old bathtub is frozen and the tadpoles are long gone, pursuing froggy futures in the swamp. Wet clothes left out on the lines are turned to cardboard.

In the morning the kitchen is a bustle of activity, full of people wrapped up in colourful skigear, warming toes by the fire or gobbling a breakfast of hot bacon and eggs at the table.

At night the dormant hot tub erupts into action, sending clouds of warm steam into the freezing air. When filled to the brim with hot, glittering water, it thaws out cold toes and hands from a day's skiing. The hot tub has been the site of many shivering and giggly grundy runs in wet togs. These are followed by a swift beating, with a rock-solid frozen t-shirt, of the people who laughed at the victim.

Late at night, when the hot tub is empty and the water gone cold, the house sheds deliciously golden light over the icy lawn and verandah. People sit around inside, sleepily basking in the warmth of the driftwood fire, playing cards or reading some of the vast collections of comics.

People always enjoy themselves at Bannockburn, no matter what the season.

ISBN 9780170195928

1 Think carefully about what you have read and see if you can work out what you think the student writer's task was. Briefly explain.

_____

_____

_____

_____

_____

2 If you came up with something along the lines of describing a particular place that the student knows well, good job. Explain how you know that the student is very familiar with this house in Bannockburn.

_____

_____

_____

_____

_____

3 No doubt you have also picked up that the student has compared the house (and surrounding area) in summer to that of winter. Carefully read through the passage again. This time note in particular the things that have been compared in both parts. You may want to use a highlighter to make it easier.

4 When we read and compare the two parts of the passage we found five direct comparisons. Using what you found out in the previous question, complete the following grid. We've done the first one for you.

Bannockburn in summer	Bannockburn in winter
The birds are so loud it sounds like a symphony orchestra.	The birds are too cold to sing their song.

ISBN 9780170195928

6   Draw the house at Bannockburn amid the surrounding environment using the details from the passage. We've given you the base to make it easier for you. Remember there are many clues to the setting that are not found in the comparisons. Read the passage carefully to help you. Also try to think of the colours and so on you would use to give your image mood.

Summer

Winter

7   Now the obvious thing would be to give it a go yourself. Think of a favourite place you have and craft a similar piece of writing. Write the final copy of your piece in the back of this book.

ISBN 9780170195928

ISBN 9780170195928

ISBN 9780170195928

ISBN 9780170195928

Use the following pages to help keep your work in one place. We suggest you use refill for any planning and drafting, and use this space for your final product. Don't forget to date and reference the appropriate unit and page number.

ISBN 9780170195928

73

ISBN 9780170195928

ISBN 9780170195928

ISBN 9780170195928

Use the following pages to help keep your work in one place. We suggest you use refill for any planning and drafting, and use this space for your final product. Don't forget to date and reference the appropriate unit and page number.

ISBN 9780170195928

ISBN 9780170195928

ISBN 9780170195928

ISBN 9780170195928

ISBN 9780170195928